.

1

The cover illustration by J.T. Blight is from Bottrell's 'Traditions and Hearthside Stories of West Cornwall' (1873). It is a depiction of 'Tom Trenoweth's Sow' which was ill-wished or begrudged by the St Buryan witch, Betty Trenoweth.

Other unlabelled inserts, and the back cover image, are from Dr. John Parkin's 'Universal Fortune Teller' of 1810. Parkin was a cunning man from Grantham in Lincolnshire. His books were advertised for sale throughout the South West.

ill-wished

Witchcraft and Magic in 19th century Cornwall

Rupert White

ANTENNA PUBLICATIONS

http://www.antennapublications.org.uk

FOREWORD

I have had a fascination with folklore and magic since my childhood but I feel it did not come into focus until I happened upon Cecil Williamson's 'Museum of Witchcraft' on the north coast of Cornwall in the 1980s. I must confess to it casting something of a spell over me. Looking back, it was not just the idiosyncratic and numinous nature of the museum itself that intrigued me but also, as a folklorist, it was the place in which the collection was situated in the whole narrative of folk magic itself. To put it bluntly ...its place was outside, on the moors with the witches!

Up until that point, what little research was in place regarding folk magic was almost entirely based on C19 folkloric records and academic literary sources. Mr Williamson was brave enough to look towards the worlds of 'material culture' and oral traditions to tell his tale, and it is not until recent times that his contribution has begun to be understood. Rupert White, too, has followed in Mr Williamson's tradition and mined rich vernacular sources to tell the haunting and still relatively untold tale of common folk living in a magical world.

I met Mr White around the same time in two separate worlds; through the world of art and at the Museum of Witchcraft and Magic. In many ways these two worlds are never that far apart! He is a medical doctor by day, but by night edits the Museum of Witchcraft and Magic journal 'The Enquiring Eye', runs artcornwall.org, and also writes extensively on folklore, popular culture and esoterica ...which, all-in-all, ideally places him for such a study. In his writings Mr White is always a 'face worker', constantly mining new raw material, and in this study he paints a picture of a people living precariously between two worlds; the world of magic and the rational world, in a not too distant, fast-changing past.

This book is neither about cursing and malefic magic, nor is it just a compendium of vintage clippings. It is a core sample of a society where the magical rubbed shoulders with the every-day. Caught between modernity and tradition, scepticism and an unflinching belief in a magical world, these accounts are sometimes moving, sometimes absurd and sometimes deeply unsettling, though all of them open a window on an aspect of our culture we have erased through a miasma of collective amnesia. For here-in lays the paradox ...for every tale of mountebankery or persecution, there lays a parallel hidden tale of an implicit belief in a coherent and complex magical world.

It is often said that in our everyday speech, it is the casual and unconsidered 'slips of the tongue' through which our true self most clearly speaks, and so too it could be said that it is through these casual and popular accounts that our inner landscape is made most explicit. Each account adds more pieces to fill the gaps in this great folk magic puzzle. In many ways Mr White's work bridges the gap between the C19 folklorists and the work of Mr Williamson, bringing us forward another 'cockstride' closer to an understanding of the Cornish folk magic tradition.

Steve Patterson
Gwithti an Pystri, Cornwall
Spring Equinox 2023

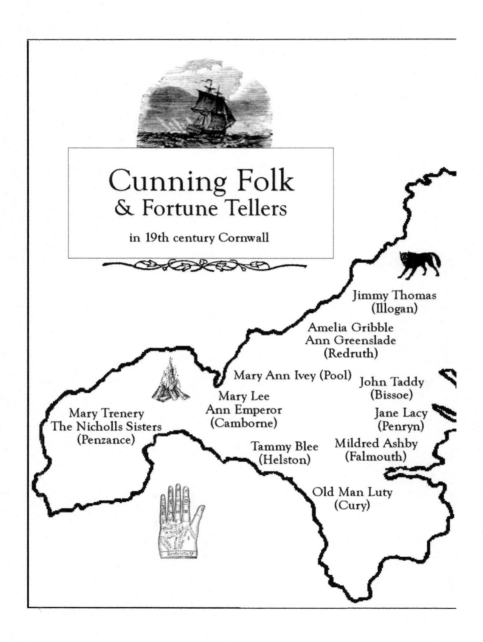

Cunning Folk
& Fortune Tellers

in 19th century Cornwall

Jimmy Thomas
(Illogan)

Amelia Gribble
Ann Greenslade
(Redruth)

Mary Ann Ivey (Pool)

John Taddy
(Bissoe)

Mary Lee
Ann Emperor
(Camborne)

Jane Lacy
(Penryn)

Mary Trenery
The Nicholls Sisters
(Penzance)

Tammy Blee
(Helston)

Mildred Ashby
(Falmouth)

Old Man Luty
(Cury)

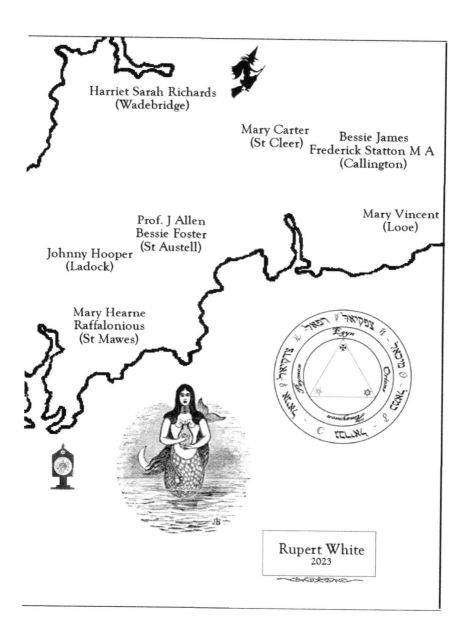

Harriet Sarah Richards
(Wadebridge)

Mary Carter
(St Cleer)

Bessie James
Frederick Statton M A
(Callington)

Prof. J Allen
Bessie Foster
(St Austell)

Mary Vincent
(Looe)

Johnny Hooper
(Ladock)

Mary Hearne
Raffalonious
(St Mawes)

Rupert White
2023

INTRODUCTION

Cunning Folk

Interest in witchcraft and in Cornish witchcraft in particular, is as strong as ever, encouraged by the continued success of the Museum of Witchcraft and Magic in Boscastle, and by Gemma Gary's writing (e.g. Gary, 2011) and imprint, Troy Books[1]. Yet there is still much that is poorly understood about it, particularly in a historical sense.

Scholarly research into witchcraft was, for several decades, preoccupied by the witch hunts of the early modern period. For a long time this had a distorting effect on perceptions of the subject, given the religious fervour and political upheavals of the era[2].

Keith Thomas' *Religion and the Decline of Magic* (1971), and, more recently, Owen Davies' series *A People Bewitched* (1999a), *Witchcraft Magic and Culture* (1999b), *Popular Magic* (2003) and *America Bewitched* (2013) have helped move the debate on, however, such that the practical, and more down-to-earth ways in which magic was used in subsequent centuries has become clearer.

The key figures here are the cunning folk who, as we shall see, were also referred to as conjurors, white witches, wizards, and in Cornwall 'pellars'. Cunning folk, whose practices remained largely unchanged from the 16th Century onwards, offered a range of magical services[3]. Using divination of various kinds, they might help recover stolen goods or lost property, or

---

[1] www.troybooks.co.uk. The growth of Modern Witchcraft in Cornwall is explored in *The Re-enchanted Landscape* (White, 2017).
[2] See Appendix F for a summary of early modern (pre-1736) witchcraft cases from Cornwall.
[3] In 1663 the bewitched 12 year old Thomas Sawdie in East Cornwall visited a cunning-man called Condy, who provided him with a bag to hang around his neck (White, 2019)

offer love magic and fortune-telling services. Most importantly, though, they could also reverse or block the effect of witchcraft - of ill-wishing, cursing or bewitchment - which tended to manifest as illness or failure to thrive in both people and animals. Indeed the dialect word 'wisht', once known widely in Cornwall, was used to describe a range of such illnesses and misfortunes[4].

Ill-wishing

There is good reason to believe that for many years there were no trained doctors in Cornwall, such that medical services in the early modern period had to be provided by well-meaning amateurs. Carew (1602) describes part-time healers - a blacksmith called Rawe Clyes and a parson, Mr Atwell - as being the most commendable. The latter, in fact, considered milk and apples as the medical treatment of choice for most conditions[5].

Certainly well into the 1800s, the treatments for all manner of illnesses were inadequate and ineffective. People who were bed-bound with depression or general malaise ('bed-lyers'), or who had strange, inexplicable illnesses, like psychosis and epilepsy, were often thought to be the victims of ill-wishing or witchcraft. Animals could, in a similar way, also suffer from being ill-wished, and therefore benefit from the same magical interventions offered by the cunning folk.

Davies (1999a) describes a related sub-group of magical practitioners. He suggests that fortune tellers, who were much more likely to be female, were not true cunning folk: they tended to offer a more limited range of services, and 'did not pretend to diagnose or cure witchcraft'.

---

whilst in 1727 William Borlase wrote to a conjuror named Bettesworth in St Ives to tell him to stop his 'meddling in the dangerous mysteries of the lower world' (Pool, P. A. S., 1986).
[4] The word is of course a contraction of 'ill-wished'. See Elworthy, F. T. (1885) The Evil Eye and White R. (2023) The Enquiring Eye (forthcoming).
[5] Heath (1750), similarly, describes a 'Society of Skilful Aunts' existing on the Isles of Scilly. This group of self-taught female healers formed, apparently, 'for want of male Practitioners in Physic'. (See White, 2019).

There is evidence of their numbers increasing during the course of the century. In 1876 a correspondent to the Cornish Telegraph said:

> ...no topography or directory of Redruth would be complete that omitted to mention the habitat of fortune-tellers, for they literally swarm here. Two of this class may be consulted at almost any hour in certain courts in the principal street, and there are oracles at East End, Buller's-row, and elsewhere in the neighbourhood.

In fact, as we shall see, many of the fortune-tellers who came before the courts claimed to be able to reverse the effects of ill-wishing and thus their practice did, in fact, overlap with that of the cunning folk[6].

Bottrell and the folklorists

What we know, or think we know, about Cornish cunning folk or 'pellars' is largely based on folklore accounts - almost exclusively Hunt (1865), Couch (1871) and Bottrell (1870, 1873, 1880) - plus odd anecdotes by Richard Polwhele, Revd Robert Hawker and A K Hamilton Jenkin[7].

Hunt's book *'Popular Romances of the West of England'* was the first to use the term 'pellar', but William Bottrell it is that provides the richest source material. The many witchcraft motifs in the three volumes of his folklore are summarised in two tables in Appendix B of this book.

There is a significant problem with 19th century folklore, however, in that the reader rarely knows the provenance, or origin, of what they are reading[8]. In the case of Bottrell, for example, it is reasonable to ask: from

---

[6] Charmers were another important sub-group of practitioner, offering an even more limited service.

[7] Jenkin in turn draws from a report by L.J.Dickinson in Old Cornwall vol2, who describes the practice of 'Old Martin', a charmer from Tintagel.

[8] This is particularly true for Robert Hunt (1865) who, rather than describe real practitioners, seems to emphasise legendary witches like the Witch of Fraddam, and the Witch of Treva. See Appendix A.

A palmist (or palm-reader) From Fortey's 'Universal Fortune Teller' (c1860)

where did he obtain his stories? Who did he speak to? How reliable were his informants, and to what extent did he make up his accounts, or embellish what he was told?

Jason Semmens underpinned the work of the folklorists by examining local registers of births, marriages and deaths to construct a biography of Tammy Blee 'The Witch of the West' (2004)[9]. He was also able to draw on research by William Paynter (1901-1976), a latter day Cornish folklorist who collected material in the 1920s and 1930s, most of which was published as newspaper articles[10].

Semmens also found an obscure, but highly illuminating, diary entry by Robert Barclay Fox (c1841), describing a visit by one of his acquaintances to see Blee:

---

[9] Blee (or Thomasine Blight 1793-1856) worked as a conjuror or cunning woman in both Redruth and Helston. As Semmens (2004) explains she moved from Back Lane West, Redruth to Helston in about 1841, and was living in Coinage Hall Street (number 46) at the time of her death in 1856.

[10] Paynter's articles have, more recently, been collated by Semmens into a single volume 'The Cornish Witch-finder' (Semmens, 2008).

In consequence of various troubles & losses, a horse & bullock, & 7 pigs feeding & not fattening, &c., on the 2nd he trudged to Redruth to consult Tammy Blee, a wise-woman or witch detector. He had to wait in a lower room from morning till dusk before his turn came, so many were the applicants for the results of her supernatural wisdom.

On being admitted, she said 'I know what you are come about', and then told him his initials, his wife's & his son's, that he was a parish officer, that he had a horse & bullock ill, which she described minutely & correctly, that he had lost a pig & that several more were doing badly, & that he had been for some time disabled from work by something in the right arm. The accuracy of all her statements made his hair stand on end & the sweat issue freely.

She further explained to him that it was all the work of an 'ill-wisher' & that there was a certain minute in every day when evil wishes took effect. She could guard him from their power, which she did by a written paper, which he was to hang around his neck &c. For his cattle she gave him powders, which he was to rub into their bodies after pulling out a few hairs, repeating during the operation, 'May the power of God keep me from evil'.

This he has done & finds them already improving. He as much believes in the power of the old lady as in the truth of any of the Gospels[11].

Semmens used a similar approach for his studies of Frederick Statton (Semmens, 2011) and Rapson Oates (Semmens, 2014)[12], and was also able to draw on some of the local newspaper articles that are included in this book, especially in the case of the latter who was often in trouble with the law.

---

[11] Jones (2020) provides another excellent anecdote regarding some stolen flour. He has also suggested that Blee lived and worked for a while in Breage, a village outside Helston.
[12] See Semmens 2011 'The Trials of Frederick Statton MA' Old Cornwall 14 no5 and Semmens 2014 'An incorrigible rogue' Old Cornwall 14 no10. Kelvin Jones' pioneering studies of Cornish witches, recently compiled into one volume (Jones, 2015) and then further updated (Jones, 2020), are a similar, if more speculative, blend of folklore, newspaper reports and historical records.

The folklorists themselves had a reciprocal relationship with the local newspapers. Hunt's *'Popular Romances'* included two articles reprinted from the West Briton (1863) about James (or Jimmey) Thomas, and another from the Western Morning News (also 1863) about Harriet King whose mother was, bizarrely, blamed for killing a cat.

Bottrell and Paynter, meantime, had a lot of their folklore material published in local papers, the former using the pen name 'Old Celt'. However, as this book shows, the overlap between the folklorists and newspapers is much less than might be expected. Only seven out of 47 (less than a 20%) magical practitioners named by the folklorists can be found mentioned in the press (see Appendix A).

The first edition of the Royal Cornwall Gazette 7.3.1801.

In addition, some well-known figures are conspicuous by their absence (e.g. Tammy Blee, though acknowledged by all the folklorists, only appears posthumously in the newspapers as the ex-wife of Jimmey Thomas). Others are portrayed very differently (e.g. Granny Boswell, rather than being 'revered for her wisdom', is frequently reported to be drunk or intimidating to others[13]).

Newspapers should really be a more objective source of information on witchcraft and magic, however, and particularly valuable if applied to the 19th century when there were many more newspaper titles in circulation. In fact most of these papers have recently been digitised, and are now searchable in the British Newspaper Archive, using relevant search terms[14].

The first paper published in Cornwall was the Tory-leaning 'Royal Cornwall Gazette' (RCG) which first appeared in 1801. The more liberal 'West Briton' arrived in 1810, and the Falmouth Packet in 1829. In total the Wikipedia page 'Media in Cornwall' lists 15 defunct papers, and another 11 current titles (see table).

The papers that appeared in the early 19th century are comparatively brief, and dominated by news from outside Cornwall. The first edition of the RCG, for example, comprises only four pages, one of which is adverts. In addition, around 90% of the news stories relate to events outside of Cornwall, being a digest or summary of stories taken from other sources.

As a consequence, stories relating to Cornish magic or witchcraft are relatively rare in the early 1800s, but become more frequent later in the century, as local newspapers become more substantial and more concentrated on Cornish news.

---

[13] See Jones, 2015
[14] For the purpose of writing this book, Cornish newspapers were searched for terms like 'bewitch', 'witchcraft' and 'ill-wish', as well as for the names of magical practitioners (eg conjuror, fortune-teller, wizard, witch etc).

Newspapers *previously* published in Cornwall	Newspapers *currently* published in Cornwall
*Royal Cornwall Gazette (1801–1951)	*The West Briton (1810)
*Falmouth Packet & Cornish Herald (1829–1848)	*Packet Newspapers (1829)
Penzance Gazette (1839–1858)	*The Cornish Times (1857)
Penzance Journal (1847–1850)	East Cornwall Times (1859)
*Cornubian (1850–1925). Between (1867–1879) called the Redruth Times	*Western Morning News (1860)
	*Cornish & Devon Post (1877)
*Cornish Telegraph (1851–1915)	*The Cornishman (1878)
*Launceston Weekly News (1856–1931)	*Cornish Guardian (1901)
*Falmouth & Penryn Weekly Times (1861–1895). Continued as Cornish Echo until 1952.	St. Ives Times & Echo (1972)
	Newquay Voice (2002)
Redruth Independent (1879–1895)	St. Austell Voice (2005)
*Cornish Post & Mining News (1889–1944)	
*St. Austell Star (1889–1915)	
St. Ives Weekly Summary (1892–1918)	
Western Echo (1899–1957)	
Newquay Express (1905–1945)	
St. Ives Times (1910–1971	

At the time of writing (Feb 2023) all the asterisked titles were searchable on the British Newspaper Archive, and were therefore used in this study.

News from elsewhere

That said, even in the Cornish newspapers, there are at least as many reports relating to witchcraft and magic from elsewhere in the UK. A striking example would be the 1863 case from Sedge Hedington in Essex, when an elderly deaf and dumb man suspected of being a witch was forcibly 'swum' in a local river, and died as a consequence a day or two later. This shocking event was reported in all the Cornish papers.

Less well covered, but just as extraordinary, in 1871 the Royal Cornwall Gazette (RCG) reported that a farmer from Cerne Abbas, Dorset believing that he had been hag-ridden, assaulted a female neighbour. He claimed that he had seen her climbing in through his bedroom window at night. Another striking account describes the magical healing of an 'imbecile' in Loch Maree in Scotland.

Occasionally reports would come from even further afield. In February 1870 it was reported that Dr David Livingstone had been killed and burnt by 'natives' in the Congo, after they had accused him of bewitching their king. The report turned out to be false. Then, in 1874, three alleged witches were burnt to death in Mexico.

Stories such as these have not, however, been included in the main text of this book, which is focussed specifically on Cornish magic and witchcraft.

A 'gallery of rogues'

Such Cornish stories are, for the most part, slightly less sensational. Instead they give a sense of folk magic used as an everyday defence against illness and misfortune. Certainly we hear of stolen money being returned, witch bottles being discovered, animal hearts being pierced and witches being scratched, alongside other less common practices.

Magical practitioners in the newspapers were all, however, vulnerable to prosecution. The laws dating from 1541, which defined witchcraft as a

From Raphael's 'Astrologer of the Nineteenth Century'

crime punishable by death were no longer in place, having been repealed and replaced by the Witchcraft Act of 1736. The new law reflected more rational attitudes to magic amongst the educated classes. It no longer accepted the reality of witchcraft, instead imposing fines or imprisonment on people who *claimed* to be able to use magical powers:

Be it enacted by the King's most Excellent Majesty...That the Statute made in the First Year of the Reign of King *James* the First, intituled, *An Act against Conjuration, Witchcaft, and dealing with evil and wicked Spirits*, shall, from the Twenty-fourth Day of *June* next, be repealed and utterly void, and of none effect...

...And for the more effectual preventing and punishing of any Pretences to such Arts or Powers as are before mentioned, whereby ignorant Persons are frequently deluded and defrauded; be it further enacted by the Authority aforesaid, That if any Person shall, from and after the said Twenty-fourth Day of *June*, pretend to exercise or use any kind of Witchcraft, Sorcery, Inchantment, or Conjuration, or undertake to tell Fortunes, or pretend, from his or her Skill or Knowledge in any occult or crafty Science, to discover where or in what manner any Goods or Chattels, supposed to have been stolen or lost, may be found, every Person, so offending, being thereof lawfully convicted on Indictment or Information in that part of *Great Britain* called *England*, or on Indictment or Libel in that part of *Great Britain* called *Scotland*, shall, for every such Offence, suffer Imprisonment by the Space of one whole Year without Bail or Mainprize....

In 1824 Parliament also passed the Vagrancy Act[15] which targeted magical practitioners in a similar way, and specifically:

'every person pretending or professing to tell fortunes, or using any subtle craft, means, or device, by palmistry or otherwise, to deceive and impose on any of his Majesty's subjects'.

Practitioners could be prosecuted using either law, especially if disgruntled customers chose to press charges. But in fact, as we shall see, in the Edwardian period many were also actively pursued by local police, who used various techniques of entrapment.

There is therefore a preponderance of stories relating to these more unscrupulous magical practitioners, who were often guilty of extorting

---

[15] Passed partly in response to homeless ex-soldiers returning from the Napoleonic Wars.

money out of vulnerable individuals. This creates a bias whereby rogues, scoundrels and other unsavoury characters become more conspicuous. Individuals that were more benign and well-liked may never have made it into newsprint. It is probably for this reason that there is a dearth of stories about charmers, for example, who evidently tended to keep out of trouble[16].

Although objective in other regards, there are also types of bias in the press linked to certain class-based assumptions. Many of the journalists are prejudiced and condescending in their tone, often referring to the clients of the magicians as uneducated, or as 'gullible dupes', and to magic and superstition as things to be violently stamped out.

Arguably this is more apparent in reports from the first half of the 19th century. As we shall see, in 1816 the ostensibly benign Ladock conjuror provoked furious indignation in the following correspondent, for example, who seems to delight in pointing out that he is illiterate: *It is extraordinary that in an age and country so enlightened as that in which we live, there should be found any persons so ignorant as to become the dupes of juggling pretenders to divination; yet so it is.*

Numerical analysis

Region	Population in 1851
Cornwall	355,558
Devon	567,098
Dorset	181,207
Somerset	443,916

The population of all four 'counties' grew between 1801 and 1891, though the last two decades saw population declines.

---

[16] Only three charms are described in the main text, but other examples are given in Appendix D.

The main text of 'ill-wished' contains 99 newspaper stories from Cornwall, a region which, during most of the 19th century, had a growing but widely dispersed population.

Over half (56) of the articles refer to the activities of a local magical practitioner, with twice as many apparently based in the west of Cornwall as the east[17]. Forty-seven articles provide the name, and other details, of the practitioner, but, as mentioned, only seven of the named individuals appear in the folklore record and so the remaining 40 have since been largely forgotten.

The majority (29 of the 47) of them are female, but the excess of women is largely accounted for by 12 individuals explicitly described as 'gipsies', who were typically working in the second half of the 19th century, or in the early 20th century.

Nearly all of the 'gipsies', rather than working from their own consulting rooms, approached people, uninvited, in their own homes. Davies (1999a) refers to them as 'door-knockers'[18]. In many cases they are shown to be manipulative and even threatening, extorting money from vulnerable clients in a way that is clearly unethical. They are described as fortune-tellers in the papers, but their approach was often to simply diagnose ill-wishing, and then to offer to lift the curse in return for money.

The majority of the ill-wishing news stories refer to humans that have been, or might be, ill-wished. Whilst most of the remainder refer to ill-wished farm animals, there are some interesting exceptions, such as an article from 1863, which describes Jimmey Thomas as being paid annually to protect ships in Hayle from witchcraft.

The remaining 43 articles do not refer to a local magical practitioner. Three involve adverts placed by fortune tellers in the latter part of the 19th century for 'astrology by post'. These fortune tellers were based in a

---

[17] With the arrival of deep mining West Cornwall became more populous. The reverse was true in the medieval period.

[18] Because they were itinerant they were less worried about having a good reputation than the sedentary or office-based practitioners would have been.

The NEW UNIVERSAL FORTUNE TELLER
By NATHAN POWELL, Doctor of Astrology
Late of the Old Baily, London.
London: Published as the Act directs, by Alexr Hogg, No. 16, Paternoster Row.

From Powell's 'Universal Fortune Teller'. The book was advertised for sale in many West Country papers eg Sherborne Mercury in the early 1800s.

number of locations outside of Cornwall. One of them, Hershell, was well known in Somerset for example (Davies, 1999a)

There are thirteen accounts of supposed witches being assaulted, typically having their blood drawn by being 'scratched'. When they result in a court case they have been referred to as 'reverse witch trials' (Davies, 1999a). The victims here all appear to have been elderly women, consistent with pre-existing witch stereotypes. There are two stories relating to witch bottles, and three relating to animal sacrifice of some kind[19].

We also see an evolution of practice. On the evidence of the articles in this book it seems that in Cornwall in the early 1800s, 'conjuror' was the preferred term for a magical practitioner. However later in the century the term 'conjuror' (like 'wizard') became more associated with stage magic[20], and partly for this reason we see the term 'fortune teller' being used much more instead.

It also seems that 'door-stepping' became more common later in the century. One possible explanation is that the work for magical practitioners was beginning to dry up, and so they had to be more proactive in looking for opportunities.

It should also be noted that there seem to have been few, if any, professional astrologers in Cornwall[21]. Davies (1999a) identified many in Somerset, particularly Bath, however, and suggests they gathered in fashionable cities of this kind, where they appealed to the more educated classes. (This is largely because astrology was more respectable and had the aura of a 'quasi-science').

---

[19] Some practices mentioned in Bottrell (see Appendix B) are not described in the newpapers, notably making curse dolls (or poppets) and burning the blood of a bewitched animal.

[20] It is striking that, after 1850, nearly all word searches for 'conjuror' in the British Newspaper Archive produce stories about stage magicians.

[21] Couch (1871), however, describes the practice of amateur astrologer John Stevens from Polperro (?) who was 'far in intellect above the ordinary conjuror and discoverer of witcheries and thefts'.

Newspaper content that is not included

Many of the Cornish newspapers featured adverts for books, and other publications. They were usually placed by their publisher, but booksellers like J. Brimmel, Launceston, E. Heard in Truro, and O. Matthews in Helston, would also advertise books for sale, as indeed would the Royal Cornwall Gazette office itself.

RCG 20.11.1813. For several years the RCG advertised and sold Moore's Almanack through its offices, and included with each sale a complimentary 'appendix'.

Universal Fortune Tellers (e.g. Powell's 'Universal Fortune Teller' (advertised in 1800) and Dr Parkin's 'Universal Fortune Teller' (advertised in 1810)) detail several techniques used for divination, including dream interpretation, palmistry (or chiromancy) and orthinomancy.

A NEW FORTUNE TELLING BOOK,
By Dr. PARKINS.

Published this Day by Tegg, 111, Cheapside, and J Poole,
Taunton. Price 2s. 6d.

THE UNIVERSAL FORTUNE TELLER,

Containing

Decrees of Fate,	Secret Writing,
Guide to Hidden Secrets,	Wheel of Fortune,
Future Events and Contin-	Art of Divination,
gencies,	Oracles by Dreams,
Astrology, Physiognomy,	Silent Language
Geomancy, Palmestry,	Mathematical Magic,
Signs by Planets, Marks, and	Curious Questions, how to
Scars,	know all Things, past,
Moles, Birds, Beasts, &c.	present, and to come,

The whole is illustrated by curious Wood Cuts, of Signs,
Figures, Planets, &c.

Where may be had,

Dr. Parkins's New Edition of Culpepper's English Herbal, 5s. bound.—The same on fine paper with coloured
plates, 7s 6d boards.

Taunton Courier and Western Advertiser 2.8.1810.

Almanacks, meanwhile, could have a range of content, but some (e.g. Raphael's Astrologer of the Nineteenth Century (advertised in 1826), Raphael's Prophetic Messenger (advertised in 1839), Zadkiel's Almanac (advertised in 1866) and Old Moore's Almanack (advertised in 1809 and later))[22] were dominated by astrology and astrological tables, and could contain other more occult content.

Interestingly both the aforementioned Universal Fortune Tellers, alongside a Vox Stellarum (Old Moore's Almanack), were found in the archives of Headon Farm, North Tamerton where they were apparently owned by the 19th century Cornish farmer Richard Palmer. This has led to speculation that this farmer was, himself, a cunning man (Langstone, 2017).

Certainly given that most cunning folk were at least semi-literate, books of this kind were, no doubt, perused by many of the magical practitioners

---

[22] Bottrell notes that Old Moore's Almanack was widely read in West Cornwall, alongside Robinson Crusoe, The Iliad and Culpeper's Herbal.

described in this book, as well as hobbyist magicians. Even if they were not actually read they could be used to furnish a cunning-man's office, or consulting rooms, in order to create the right 'mystical' ambience - (see e.g. entry for John Taddy, 'Wizard of the West' 1903).

Fashionable 'white magic'

In 1888 some of the Cornish papers reported on a show-day given by Newlyn Artists. Painter Stanhope Forbes, apparently, displayed three works, one of which was entitled 'Palmistry': *"Palmistry,"...is destined for the Exhibition of the English Art Club...There are only two figures, those of a lady; and gentleman - lovers perhaps. They have left the crowded ball-room for the secluded nook in which they sit, and are indulging in a little of that harmless form of "white magic" which is so fashionable just now.*

RCG 6.11.1824 Advert by publisher W Charlton Wright for Raphael's colourful 'Astrologer of the Nineteenth Century'.

A 'palmistry tent' manned by amateur enthusiasts, alongside a raffle, cake stalls and Punch and Judy regularly featured as a side-show at a number of village fetes and bazaars in Cornwall in the 1890's.

Although most thought it harmless, not all did. On Feb 6th 1902 the West Briton published a letter by a concerned parishioner from Lostwithiel who, on moral grounds, condemned the church for raising money using clairvoyance, palmistry, fortune telling and such methods.

However, articles describing magic - including palmistry - as amateur entertainment are also not included in the main text of this book. Nor is stage magic, which was first reported in the RCG in 1807 when Moon, the great conjuror, 'surprised the West of England with his deceptions and sleight of hand &c'[23].

---

[23] The Royal Cornwall Gazette (RCG) had, later, to explain that 'Moon the great conjuror' was not the same person as 'Moon the great astronomer and editor of the Western Almanack'

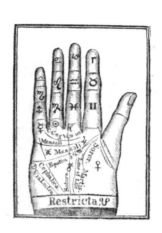

29

NEWSPAPER ARTICLES

Terrified thief, Sithney (1802)

several per-
ten and half
derable steep-
s in an hour,
: rate of eight
ave our infor-
:d respectable
at the time ;
suasion of the
projectors are
tent to secure

y is now rais-
anded by Ed-
tention of this

Mr. Gendell, took the child to his house, and
has adopted it into his own family.

About a fortnight since, was stolen fr m
the dwelling-house of John Hockin (labourer)
of the parish of Sithney, a small bag, containing cash to the amount of about 10l. the
property of his son. Suspicion having fallen
on two or three of the neighbours, a warrant
was procured, and their houses searched, but
to no effect.—The young man, however, unwilling to give up his money without some
further research, resolved last Saturday to go
to the *Conjurer*, and declared his intention to
some of the neighbours of going the next
morning. Superstition effected what honesty

RCG 20.2.1802

About a fortnight since, was stolen from the dwelling-house of John
Hockin (labourer) of the parish of Sithney, a small bag, containing cash to
the amount of about 10l., the property of his son.

Suspicion having fallen on two or three of the neighbours, a warrant was
procured, and their houses searched, but to no effect. -The young man,
however, unwilling to give up his money without some further research,
resolved last Saturday to go to the Conjurer[24], and declared his intention
to some of the neighbours of going the next morning. Superstition
effected what honesty could not; the terrified thief, in the course of the
night, brought back 6 guineas (perhaps all that was left) and dropped it in
at the door of the house whence it was taken, to the joy of the family, who
found it in the morning.

---

[24] Sithney is very close to Helston, where the conjuror was probably based. They may well
be the male 'pellar' described by Bottrell (1870) as 'renewing Capt Mathey's protection'
(Appendix B). Certainly, whether male or female, they must have preceded Tammy Blee,
who was only 9 in 1802 (b. 1793). Blee moved to Helston much later - in 1841.
Interestingly the St Ives conjuror rebuked in the 1727 letter by William Borlase (see
footnote 3) also specialised in recovering lost and stolen goods (Pool, 1986).

Mare burnt to death, St Martin's (1802)

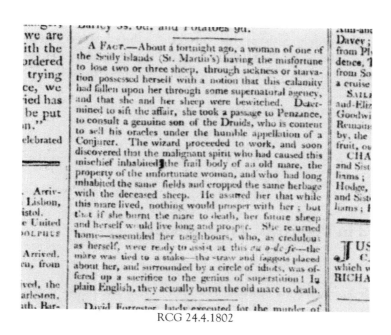

RCG 24.4.1802

A FACT - About a fortnight ago, a woman of one of the Scilly islands (St. Martin's) having the misfortune to lose two or three sheep, through sickness or starvation possessed herself with a notion that this calamity had fallen upon her through some supernatural agency, and that she and her sheep were bewitched. Determined to sift the affair, she took a passage to Penzance, to consult a genuine son of the Druids, who is content to sell his oracles under the humble appellation of a Conjurer.

The wizard proceeded to work, and soon discovered that the malignant spirit who had caused this mischief inhabited the frail body of an old mare, the property of the unfortunate woman, and who had long inhabited the same fields and cropped the same herbage with the deceased sheep. He assured her that while this mare lived, nothing would prosper with her; but that if she burnt the mare to death, her future sheep and herself would live long and prosper.

She returned home-assembled her neighbours, who, as credulous as herself, were ready to assist at this auto-de-fe[25] - the mare was tied to a stake - the straw and faggots placed about her, and surrounded by a circle of idiots, was offered up a sacrifice to the genius of superstition!

In plain English, they actually burnt the old mare to death.

Wizard in Petticoats, Truro (1806)

This rather convoluted article appeared in the Truro news section of 1806. It seems to describe an androgynous travelling fortune-teller who offered to avert the 'evil' of a child born out of wedlock by using magic. The magic required the use of the still-warm underclothes of a local girl.

A travelling *witch*, or as some believe, a *wizard* in petticoats, has lately made *a shift* to *raise the wind* among certain credulous young misses in this neighbourhood, in a way that has afforded no little merriment to their laughter-loving neighbours. The *bearded sybil* told fortunes; and when the confiding votery thought of nothing but a handsome or rich husband, she was thunderstruck with the prediction of having " a baby for her cradle, before

RCG 20.12.1806

---

[25] Act of Faith

A travelling *witch*, or as some believe, a *wizard* in petticoats, has lately made *a shift* to *raise the wind* among certain credulous young misses in this neighbourhood, in a way that has afforded no little merriment to their laughter-loving neighbours.

The bearded Sybil told fortunes; and when the confiding votery thought of nothing but a handsome or rich husband, she was thunderstruck with the prediction of having "a baby for her cradle, before she had a husband for her bed". To avert this dire disgrace, the conjuror was intreated to use his most potent spells. But this the oracle of the fates declared to be impossible unless the fair unfortunate would strip off the shift from her body and delivered it warm to the *seer*, who engaged to sacrifice it to the moon, at midnight, with such "horrid mysteries" as would not fail to avert the dreaded evil. They stripped; - but whether he-she conjuror has been caught up into the moon, or has flown on a broom-stick to Lapland to bleach the linen, certain it is, that neither conjuror or linen have since appeared.

The Ladock Conjuror (1808)

The following report was exported to newspapers across the country, and prompted some correspondence reproduced in Polwhele's 'Traditions and Recollections' Vol.2 (1826) [26].

A blacksmith named Samuel Cornish, living at Twelve Heads, in Kenwyn near Truro, on Saturday night last, fell into a shaft of Creegbraws mine above seven fathom deep, where he continued till Tuesday morning, when he was taken out, so little injured, as to be able to walk home apparently unhurt; and, extraordinary as it may appear, he declared that during his abode in the shaft he experienced neither hunger nor thirst. But a more wonderful fact still remains to be told. Having been missed all Sunday, by his family and neighbours, on Monday they repaired to the celebrated *Ladock conjuror!* who informed them, it seems that the object of their search was alive and well, sitting upon a stone in the bottom of a shaft, and that if they were industrious in their search and hit upon the right shaft before Tuesday noon, they would take him out alive. A *posse* of the *faithful,* accordingly proceeded in the search, and completely verified the prediction of the conjuror!

RCG 30.1.1808

A blacksmith named Samuel Cornish, living at Twelve Heads, in Kenwyn near Truro, on Saturday night last, fell into a shaft of Creegbraws mine above seven fathom deep, where he continued till Tuesday morning, when he was taken out, so little injured, as to be able to walk home apparently unhurt; and, extraordinary as it may appear, he declared that during his abode in the shaft he experienced neither hunger nor thirst.

---

[26] Polwhele comments: *The voice from Ladock is still oracular. Money of a great amount has been often recovered through its influence. I witnessed once, myself, the restoration of 20 guineas to the place whence they had been stolen, by a wretch who feared the conjuror more than any justice of the quorum. During the last fifty years, however, superstition has been gradually losing ground in every neighbourhood; though here and there we meet with a strong feature of it. Within my remembrance, there were conjuring parsons and cunning clerks, every blacksmith was a doctor and every old woman was a witch...*

But a more wonderful fact still remains to be told. Having been missed all Sunday, by his family and neighbours, on Monday they repaired to the celebrated Ladock conjuror who informed them, it seems that the object of their search was alive and well, sitting upon a stone in the bottom of a shaft, and that if they were industrious in their search and hit upon the right shaft before Tuesday upon, they would take him out alive. A posse of the faithful, accordingly proceeded in the search, and completely verified the prediction of the conjuror!

Robbery and Conjuration, St Austell (1809)

The following year, in 1809, a reclusive father and son from St Austell, who had £400 saved in a chest, returned home to find it gone. We learn in the RCG that, in order to recover it, they went to a local conjuror. Given Ladock is only 5 or so miles from St Austell this, too, is likely to have been the Ladock Conjuror.

On Monday morning the old man and his son rose early; the former to repair to his conjurorship, and the latter to flee from the impending calamity. On reaching their gate, to their great astonishment, they found a quantity of silver coin strewed on the ground, to attract their notice. On picking it up, to their great joy they discovered close by the post of the gate, the bag which contained their absent gold not one piece of which had been " embezzled or mislaid." The journey of course was laid aside, and the neighbourhood was saved from the storm.—The thief, it seems, who did not hesitate to violate the laws of his country, had not fortitude enough to brave the power of the cunning-man—If the name of conjurer can work such miracles, what must not the conjurer himself be able to accomplish?

RCG 22.4.1809

35

...Saturday was spent in lamentations over the departed gold, Sunday in contriving how to recover it...No method was left but to apply to the conjurer. On this they resolved; and Monday morning was the time fixed for the old man to go to relate his tale, and place confidence in his art.

We do not pretend to know, where this conjuror lives: but his power is well known. A discovery of the thief was considered inevitable, and his punishment was to be in proportion to the magnitude of the offence. The son, in the meanwhile, prepared to retire at a distance, as Lot departed from Sodom, that he might escape the dreadful effects of the thunders, lightnings, and demons, which on the succeeding days were to mingle together, recover the stolen money, and transfix the thief with vengeance.

This report was circulated, and fully credited by many. On Monday morning the old man and his son rose early; the former to repair to his conjurorship, and the latter to flee from the impending calamity. On reaching their gate, to their great astonishment, they found a quantity of silver coin strewed on the ground, to attract their notice. On picking it up, to their great joy they discovered close by the post of the gate, the bag which contained their absent gold not one piece of which had been "embezzled or mislaid."

The journey of course was laid aside, and the neighbourhood was saved from the storm. - The thief, it seems, who did not hesitate to violate the laws of his country, had not fortitude enough to brave the power of the cunning-man. - If the name of conjurer can work such miracles, what must not the conjurer himself be able to accomplish?

Johnny Hooper, alias The Laddock Conjurer (1816)

In 1816, eight years after the Ladock Conjurer located Samuel Cornish in the mineshaft, the following article by 'W. W.' appeared in the West Briton. It provides the conjuror's birth name, and gives us some interesting insights into his practice:

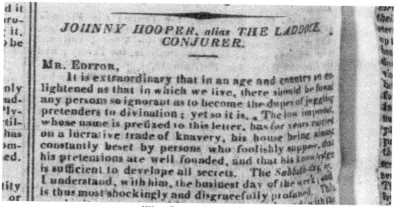

West Briton 21.6.1816

JOHNNY HOOPER, alias THE LADOCK CONJURER

MR. EDITOR,
It is extraordinary that in an age and country so enlightened as that in which we live, there should be found any persons so ignorant as to become the dupes of juggling pretenders to divination; yet so it is.

The low imposter, whose name is prefixed to this letter, has for years carried on a lucrative trade of knavery, his house bring almost constantly beset by persons who foolishly suppose, that his pretensions are well founded, and that his knowledge is sufficient to develop all secrets.

37

The Sabbath-day is I understand, with him, the busiest day of the week; and is thus most shockingly and disgracefully profaned. This oracle, it seems, can neither write nor read, and (with the exception of a little low cunning) his ignorance is only to be exceeded by that of those who apply to him. His oracles, like those of the Pythoness of Delphos are delivered with the greatest ambiguity, and seldom differ from the suspicions of the applicant.

Should any request to see the face of the person who has robbed them, or who is supposed to have brought calamities upon them by ill wishes, the impostor puts them to look upon an old stopper of a decanter, which gives an indistinct reflection of the face, that may be easily converted into the likeness of the suspected person. Thousands have proved the futility of his pretensions; and still, though his method of necromancy is so glaringly absurd, he is followed by ignorant multitudes.

He seems aware that by the practice of his art, he exposes himself to legal punishment, and therefore enjoins secrecy on all who apply to him. It is hoped that some active Magistrate will interfere, to put a stop to the depredations of this swindler, who every week succeeds in levying contributions on a number of simpletons, many of whom, from their appearance, should be supposed to know better.

I am, Sir, &c. W. W.

Robbery at Davidstowe (1828)

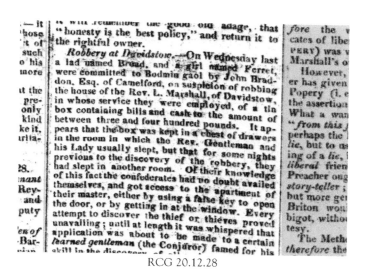

RCG 20.12.28

Davidstowe is more than 20 miles from Ladock. This is, therefore, likely to be a different conjuror based nearer Camelford.

On Wednesday last a lad named Broad, and girl named Ferret, were committed to Bodmin gaol by John Braddon, Esq. of Camelford, on suspicion of robbing the house of the Rev. L. Marshall, of Davidstowe, whose service they were employed, of a tin box containing bills and cash to the amount of between three and four hundred pounds....

...Every attempt to discover the thief or thieves proved unavailing; until at length it was whispered that application was about to be made to a certain *learned gentleman* (the Conjuror) famed for his skill in the discovery of all such delinquents. This threatened appeal to the powers of darkness produced it seems the desired effect upon the mind of the juvenile depredators...

Abstracted sovereigns, Lanivet (1829)

West Briton 25.9.29

The following article in the West Briton suggests that Johnny Hooper, a.k.a. the Ladock Conjuror, was still active in 1829[27]:

A poor man named John Rowe, who resides at Tremoor, in the parish of Lanivet, and who is far advanced in life, had by industry and economy scraped together twenty pounds, which he converted into sovereigns and put in a box, the key of which he always kept in his possession.

On Sunday last he went to add something to his store, and on counting over his treasure, he observed that the pieces were not all alike. This led to a scrutiny, when he discovered that 16 of the sovereigns had been abstracted, and 14 farthings, a shilling and a button without a shank, all covered with leaf gold, put in their stead. The poor man is in the greatest distress at being thus deprived of the savings of a long life; he suspects a particular individual of the theft, but in place of instituting an inquiry

---

[27] A fifth article, this time in the RCG 1835 mentions the 'recent demise' of John Hooper Esq of Ladock. Parish records for Ladock confirm that Hooper died in 1833 at the advanced age of 87 (d.o.b. 1746).

through a Magistrate, he has resolved to apply to a conjuror called "Johnny Hooper," to ascertain if his suspicions are well founded, in the hope that some part of the money may be restored through the influence of the cunning man.

Witch's Tower, Launceston (1833)

The Witch's Tower, Launceston, was so-named because it was thought to be the site of a witch execution (c.f. Courtney, 1890) [28].

Witch's Tower, Launceston Castle.

---

[28] Relevant here is the following anecdote: 14th Nov 1851 RCG: *'The late Rev Arundell informed me that in order to test the truth of this tradition he had dug out some of the earth and rubbish and discovered the staple to which a chair had been affixed together with evident marks of combustion'* (see Jones, 2020). However, his experiment was flawed: in England and in most English speaking countries, of course, witches were hanged not burnt.

During the night of Tuesday last this County was visited by a most violent storm which continued throughout the whole of Wednesday and part of the following night. Much damage has been done to the roofs and walls of houses chimneys have been down &c. but we have not heard of any lives being lost.

At Launceston the "witches tower" of the old castle, we understand, was blown down and a great many houses in that town as well as the orchards in the neighbourhood have sustained material injury...

Satan's agents, St Ewe (1836)[29]

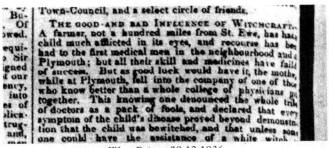

West Briton 28.10.1836

THE GOOD AND BAD INFLUENCE OF WITCHCRAFT.
A farmer, not hundred miles from St. Ewe, has had a child much afflicted in its eyes, and recourse has been had to the first medical men in the neighbourhood and in Plymouth; but all their skill and medicines have failed of success. But as good luck would have it, the mother while at Plymouth fell into the company of one of those who know better than a whole college of physicians together. This knowing one denounced the whole tribe of doctors as a pack of fools, and declared that every symptom

---

[29] St Ewe is a few miles south of St Austell. This story is referenced in Jones, 2015.

of the child's disease proved beyond demonstration that the child was bewitched, and that unless someone could have the assistance of a white witch to expel the influence of the black witch, the child would never recover.

This person likewise informed the mother that there was one of the former description who resided in Plymouth, who no doubt would cure her child. The poor mother returned home, and laid the whole affair open to her husband, who, from the impulse of love to his child, and wishing to wreak his vengeance on the black witch, declared that he would spend the last farthing he had in the world to find out the author of this mischief, and to have his child cured. A friend was sent off immediately to Plymouth to seek out the white witch and to bring her without delay, whatever might be the expense. The witch, not like those in olden time who took their journeys on broomsticks, came by coach and soon after refreshment, all the paraphernalia of the occult science were put into operation; and in a few days the important matter was brought to a crisis.

She could not counteract what the black witch had done, but had put a stop to all future influence, and moreover gave the parents a clear idea who was the author of the child's illness. So now woe betide the guilty. Her blood may pay the penalty of her crimes, or a less punishment may be awarded by a good ducking in a horse pond. Thus far immense good has been done. Witchcraft has been arrested and the witch discovered.

Still it is feared that the benefit received will not counterbalance the mischief done. Many firmly believe that the witch, in her journey from Plymouth, raised the late severe storm, for it was observed that, on the road as she came, houses were unroofed and trees torn up by their roots. The authorities at Plymouth are earnestly intreated to find out the author of all this mischief, to confine her to her own town, and not allow her to go abroad raising storms, and thereby injuring whole nations merely to benefit a few. Let people carry their bewitched subjects to Plymouth and not raise hurricanes by conveying Satan's agents from one part of the nation to another (From a Correspondent).

Bewitched Seine (1840)

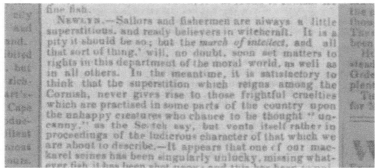

RCG 22.5.1840

NEWLYN.-Sailors and fishermen are always a little superstitious and ready believers in witchcraft. It is a pity it should be so; but the march of intellect, and all that sort of thing will, no doubt, soon set matters to rights in this department of the moral world, as well as in all others...
...It appears that one of our mackerel seines[30] has been singularly unlucky, missing whatever fish it has been shot upon; and this has been so uniformly the case, that it was thought it could not be owing to accident. The evil was therefore laid at the door of a poor young woman of weak intellect, who perhaps might, upon the provocations to which such unfortunate people are too often exposed, have given way to the practice of ill wishing.

But instead of burning the witch, the aggrieved party applied the purifying influence of fire to the object of her supposed malevolence; and on Monday last a part of the seine was burnt, amid the acclamations of a large crowd of spectators!

We hope this remedy will prove effectual and that next week we shall have to record an abundant catch of fish by the disenchanted net...

---

[30] A seine net is fishing net that hangs vertically in the water with its bottom edge held down by weights and its top edge buoyed by floats.

RCG 29.5.1840

As promised the paper reported back the following week:

PENZANCE - the seine which had been bewitched at Newlyn, appears to have been thoroughly disenchanted by the process which we described last week, and has since been blessed with singular good luck.

Before it had undergone the sort of exorcism practised upon it, it never caught any fish; and now it seems never to miss them: so that, in the course of the week, it has taken no less than 70l or 80l worth. This shows how much better it is to smoke the Devil out of any inanimate object into which he may have insinuated himself, than to attack him in the person of the witch, whose bidding he may be supposed to have obeyed; that being a strong hold which be never relinquishes except in the last extremity.

Not a hundred miles from Tywardreath (1841)[31]

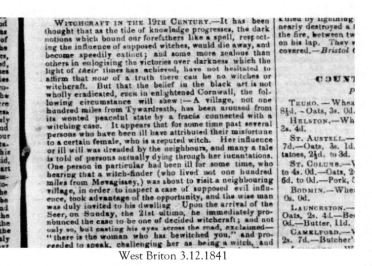

West Briton 3.12.1841

WITCHCRAFT IN THE 19TH CENTURY. – It has been thought that as the tide of knowledge progresses, the dark notions which bound our forefathers like a spell, respecting the influence of supposed witches, would die away, and become speedily extinct; and some more zealous than others in eulogising the victories over darkness which the light of their times has achieved, have not hesitated to affirm that now of a truth there can be no witches or witchcraft. But that the belief in the black art is not wholly eradicated, even in enlightened Cornwall, the following circumstance will show: -

A village, not one hundred miles from Tywardreath[32], has been aroused from its wonted peaceful state by a fracas connected with a witching case. It appears that for some time past several persons who have been ill have

---

[31] This article features in *The Folklore of Cornwall* by Deane and Shaw (1975).
[32] If not Par or St Blazey, then this village could be Tywardreath itself (see 'Death of a Cornish Witch' (1880)).

attributed their misfortune to a certain female, who is a reputed witch. Her influence or ill will was dreaded by the neighbours, and many a tale is told of persons actually dying through her incantations. One person in particular had been ill for some time, who hearing that a witch-finder (who lived not one hundred miles from Mevagissey,) was about to visit a neighbouring village, in order to inspect a case of supposed evil influence, took advantage of the opportunity, and the wise man was duly invited to his dwelling.

Upon the arrival of the Seer, on Sunday, the 21st ultimo[33], he immediately pronounced the case to be one of decided witchcraft; and not only so, but casting his eyes across the road, exclaimed- "there is the woman who has bewitched you," and proceeded to speak, challenging her as being a witch, and the author of the evil which the patient suffered. Upon this the woman flew at him, and a desperate conflict ensued, when it is supposed that the woman inflicted a slight wound on her throat, in order to charge the Seer with attempting her life.

The case of assault and battery was a subject for investigation by the powers above them on the coming Monday, when persons hesitated not to charge her with practising witchery for some the past, to the injury of life and limb. One of the witnesses, it appeared, had attended on the woman some months since, when ill, when she declared, as she wished to die easy, the way and manner of her initiation into the mystery of witchcraft, which was by attending the sacrament, and repeating the Lord's prayer thrice backwards, partaking of the wine, but securing the bread, and giving it to a toad[34], which, according to the prediction of her instructress, she found on her way home, and took with her and retained as the magic power of her spell.

Whether she has resigned this personification of the demon of the black art, we have not been informed; but we should suppose that the good folks of that enlightened locality would not be satisfied with such a formidable monster existing among them in all its malignant potency.

---

[33] Last month

[34] i.e. whilst ill, and fearing imminent death, she confessed that she became a witch after saying the Lord's Prayer backwards, and feeding the communion wafer (or bread) to a toad.

From her confession, however, it appeared that she at that time would fain yield up her power, but with the return of health the witching was not laid aside-thus bearing out the old ditty,

> "When the devil was ill, the devil a monk would be
> But when the devil got well, the devil a monk was he."

Evidence was gone into of her being in the constant habit of using violent language towards persons, and otherwise rendering herself generally obnoxious, and on this count (for upon a charge of witchery who would convict?)- she was held to bail to keep the peace for two years. The sick man, in the meantime, recovered, but strong fears are entertained that although debarred from using ill language, she may exercise the power which she possesses for mischief in a silent manner, to the further injury of her Majesty's subjects in that district.

It is strange that when once a person has the reputation of being a witch, prejudice is so strong that it is with great difficulty one convert to reason can be gained from amongst those who are prejudiced. Much has been said of the march of intellect, but there are many places where her sway is considered as of secondary importance in comparison with the fostering of that bane of all that is great and good- superstition. Let the notion of witchcraft be but encouraged, and persons will not be wanting to take advantage of the unreasonable belief, either for the purpose of making themselves feared, or for a private advantage.- Where is the schoolmaster?

Looe Superstition and Knavery (1842)

RCG 16.12.1842

LOOE.- *Superstition and Knavery*. –At Sandplace, near Looe, about a fortnight since, two Gipsy women, styling themselves fortune tellers, entered the house of William Pearce, who was at the time unwell, and labouring under the impression that he was bewitched.

After a little conversation between them and Mrs. Pearce, they offered to restore her husband to perfect health, by her raising all the money she possibly could, which amounted to 16l. 4s. 6d. The fortune tellers in question went through the necessary process for rendering the ill-wishes of the witch of no avail, and then pretending to lock the money up for three days and securing the key in their own possession, decamped with the promise of returning at the appointed time.

Shortly after their departure suspicion arose in the mind of a junior branch of the family, upon which the box was broken open, when to their great astonishment and dismay, instead of finding the 16l. 4s. 6d., only 24d. was left. The fugitives were immediately pursued by Mr. Wynhall, of

Looe, constable and after a chase of eight miles he succeeded in coming up with the delinquents, as well as a man who had joined them. After a desperate struggle with the man, who is an exceedingly powerful fellow, he took from his person 15l. 3s. 6d.

The women, amidst the conflict between Mr Wynhall and the man, made their escape. After the man had undergone an examination before the Rev. R. Bull of Lanreath, by whom he was committed for trial, he subsequently effected his escape from custody, and has never since been heard of. The money still remains in the hands of Mr. Wynhall.

St Germoe Conjuror (1842)

SORCERY. – A thrifty woman in the neighbourhood of Truro having been robbed last week of three sovereigns walked down to Germoe to consult a conjuror who once lived there[35]. He had been gathered to his father but it seems had left his mantle with his daughter who according to

---

[35] Truro to St Germoe, Penzance is a distance of nearly 30 miles.

her art eased the poor woman of 2s. and requested her to come again. On her return home she was recommended to a Mrs.___ of Redruth whose name will be exposed if she does not relinquish her practice.

The silly creature went on a second pilgrimage to this Sibyl, who took her fee and then required a shilling for the purpose of her art "to be burnt to ashes" (as she was afterwards told by the sorceress) "to prick the conscience of the robber" – Why will not people put their money in the Savings Bank?

Frederick Statton, M.A., Callington (1843)[36]

CONJUROR AND NO CONJURORS.—At the Cornwall Assizes last week a fortune teller named Frederick Peter Statton, who on his paper apologies for cards styles himself with great truth a Master of Arts, was tried on four several indictments for practising on the superstition of his neighbours. The victim whose case was first taken was Jenny Francis, wife of James Francis, a labourer at Stokeclimsland. Jenny's heifer strayed from the Common, and Jenny went to the cunning man for directions to find it. He took down a slate and cast up something, and then told her the heifer had strayed fourteen miles to the south-east, and moreover that she was with calf. Jenny paid him his demand, three shillings, for the news, and sent her husband 14 miles to the south east to find the heifer, but poor Jemmy went on a fool's errand, for the heifer was found a mile and half to the north-east: and double shame to the ...

RCG 7.4.1843

---

[36] Hunt (1865) describes a man that fits Statton's description appearing before the board of the asylum asking for them to place an 'imbecile' girl in his care. Apparently from Callington, he referred to himself as a 'Master of the Black Arts'. Semmens (2011) identifies Statton's home as being 'Solomon's Temple' in St Dominic a mile east of Callington.

This case, heard before the Assize courts, was widely reported, especially across Bristol and the South West. Other journalists, who are equally condescending, describe Statton as a 'great country-looking bumpkin', or as 'a chubby dumpling-faced looking fellow'. They also report that two other indictments were considered but rejected by the court, including an attempt by Statton to recover stolen goods.

CONJUROR AND NO CONJURORS. – At the Cornwall assizes last week a fortune teller named Frederick Peter Statton, who on his paper apologies for cards styles himself with great truth 'a Master of Arts', was tried on four separate indictments for practising on the superstition of his neighbours.

The victim whose case was first taken in was *Jenny Francis*, wife of James Francis, a labourer at Stokeclimsland. Jenny's heifer strayed from the Common and Jenny went to the cunning man for directions to find it. He took down a slate and cast up something and then told her the heifer had strayed 14 miles to the southeast, and moreover, that she was with calf. Jenny paid him his demand, three shillings, for the news and sent her husband 14 miles to the southeast to find the heifer. But poor Jenny went on a fool's errand for the heifer was found a mile and a half to the northeast, and double shame to the deceiver, he proved not to be with calf at all.

Mr Slade, the prisoner's counsel availed himself very ably of all the ridiculous points of the case. But his jokes, however provocative of merriment in the court, would have little availed his client, if he had not shown that the indictment was bad. The jury acquitted him under the judge's direction with great reluctance.

The prisoner who was only 23 years of age[37], called one of the jury to give him a character. This witness's evidence was of a very negative kind. He had known Statton almost ever since he could (remember), never knew him keep an evil spirit. Never had anything to do with him. Cannot tell much about his character. Has heard that when people have lost anything

---

[37] Frederick Statton was thus still a very young man, and new to his work as a 'Master of Arts' when he made this court appearance. According to Semmens (2011) he was born in 1820, but died in 1854 at the age of only 34.

they go to him cannot tell how he gets his living. Never saw him working his life.

The next prosecutor was a farmer of Stokeclimsland named Nottle, who certainly appeared to be very unfurnished in the noddle, and seemed rather to belong to the ancient and respectable family of the noodles. This person went to the Master of Arts in January last year in consequence of three of his cattle dying in a strange manner in 10 days, and another ill as well as several fat sheep.

Statton told him he could put him to rights; that he should not lose any more cattle. Upon this assurance Nottle desired him to proceed. Statton said he would do it, that Nottle was ill wished, but he should not lose any more cattle. He took a slate and drew a figure as in Moore's Almanack[38] and in about 10 minutes repeated that Nottle was ill wished. He would not tell the name of the person, but would so describe his features, size, and what he was that he should be known. He then gave directions how to know the person who had ill wished him which Nottle read in court: - *Take the calf and kill it. Take the heart out and prick it full of pins. On Thursday morning next, at the first hour the sun rises, put the heart into a fire and roast or burn it to ashes. The person's name you suspect of ill-wishing you must be written on a piece of paper and put in the heart with the pins run through the name. During the time the heart is roasting the 35th Psalm must be read three times.*

After this Nottle asked what was to pay to which the conjuror replied, he had been accustomed to charge a pound but would charge a him only 10 shillings, which not all paid him. The jury immediately found the prisoner guilty. But his counsel Mr. Slade moved in arrest of judgement, and the result was that he escaped on technical objections from all the indictments, the judge gave him a severe admonition, assuring him that though he had now been known, so fortunate as to escape, he would find that if he continued his bad practices, the law is strong enough to reach in credulity.

---

[38] Old Moore's Almanack, or Vox Stellarum, includes moon phases and similar astrological calculations, and has been published annually since 1697.

West Briton 14.4.1848

Five years later, in 1848, Statton was back in the news, having escaped from prison:

SINGULAR AFFRAY AT CALLINGTON.-An affray took place at Kit Hill, on Saturday last, between a man called Frederick Statton and two constables and their three assistants. Statton, a few months ago, was committed to Bodmin gaol for poaching on the property of Augustus Coryton, Esq., but finding the gaol door open one day, he took the liberty of walking off before the time of his discharge arrived.

Since then all the constables in Cornwall have been on the look-out for him, but have been baffled in all their attempts to retake him. Bullen, one of the Callington constables, managed to get in the same room with him one day, but Statton vanished without Bullen knowing how, and Statton being a conjuror, was supposed to have made his egress through the key-hole. But it appears that a man called Thomas Penaluna has been a confidant of Statton's, they being engaged together in Kit Hill mine. Penaluna happening to be at the Bodmin assizes, heard the turnkey offer a reward of 5l. to anyone who would bring Statton to him, which Penaluna accepted, and thereupon instructed Dawe, a constable of Liskeard, and Bullen, the Callington constable, to meet him at Kit Hill on Saturday, and to bring two or three assistants with them. He then wrote to Statton a very friendly note inviting him to Kit Hill to see some tin stuff which had lately been raised there. Statton, thereupon, went to Kit Hill with his brother, who took a gun with him to shoot anything that might happen to fall in his way. When Penaluna got them in the round-house to see the tin, he got out and turned the key on them, and called the constables, who were lying in a pit hard by, when Bullen came up. He said, "Ah, Mr. Statton, can you get through the keyhole now?" Statton said no, he would surrender. They then opened the door; out flew Statton, with a sword in his hand, and cut his way through the whole, and, it appears, made an aim at Bullen's head. He, fortunately, parried the blow with his arm, and received a cut. The brother said he would shoot them; but they succeeded in taking the gun from him. Statton, however, ran off like a greyhound, and the constables after him; but both he and his brother have for the time given them the slip.-

Churchyard ritual, Phillack (1844)

WITCHCRAFT IN 1844.—Not long since, the resting place of the dead, at Phillack, near Hayle, was made the scene of transactions which would have blackened the darkest ignorance of bygone ages. It appears that several persons who are afflicted with disease, and who, for want of moral courage, would not submit to the directions of their medical advisers, very readily caught hold of and applied every nostrum that gossips made known. Experience proving that the boasted remedies were of no avail, their imaginations were put to the utmost stretch, in order that they might avoid the only method by which they could be cured. Fortunately, a

West Briton 6.9.1844

WITCHCRAFT IN 1844. - Not long since, the resting place of the dead, at Phillack, near Hayle, was made the scene of transactions which would have blackened the darkest ignorance of bygone ages.

It appears that several persons who are afflicted with disease, and who, for want of moral courage, would not submit to the directions of their medical advisers, very readily caught hold of and applied every nostrum that gossips made known. Experience proving that the boasted remedies were of no avail, their imaginations were put to the utmost stretch, in order that they might avoid the only method by which they could be cured.

Fortunately, a blazing light shot across their darkened way, and their gloomy reflections were dissipated by its brilliancy. It was a revelation; and they denounced their ignorance, because they did not sooner find out the cause of their malady. To believe that they were ill-wished was only the work of a moment, but to discover a person who could break the spell was not so easily accomplished. Every thought and action was centered in attaining their darling object. Finally, their wish was consummated, and a scatterer of witch spells stalked forth from Helston[39], to whom they disclosed every incident of their lives, fraught with uncertainty as tending to good or evil.

The day was chosen, the dreaded hour of midnight fixed, and the abode of the silent clod of all that once was living was named as the place of assignation. The hour drew near, but their purpose became known from the impulse of their ecstasies, and their stealthy actions were closely watched. The asked-for fee was immediately given, and after silence was enjoined, the church-yard wall was scaled. Then the spell-breaker commenced the mysteries of his art, by making mysterious sounds and performing mysterious actions, as he walked over the dead, hotly pressed by his frightened dupes. Having walked many times around the church, the doors and windows opened and shut at his bidding. Then he commanded them to remain open, and as they were passed in succession, he brought the persons who had ill-wished them to their face.

Thus the spell was broken and dissolved, and a faith given that their cure would be speedily effected. Some days have since elapsed, and either their faith has failed, or the witch-spell is not broken, for their disease still maintains its ground, the effect of a visible cause.

---

[39] Tammy Blee set up shop in Helston in about 1841. This 1844 article, together with an earlier one (see entry for 1802) suggests that there was also a male pellar active in Helston in the early 19th century. Bottrell (1870), famously, describes a comical ritual in Stithians churchyard that involved Blee (see Appendix B).

The Blood of Hannah Rodda (1844)

RCG 27.9.1844

*Thought to have been a witch, in 1844 Hannah Rodda of Helston was assaulted by Mary
Edwards on the advice of Mrs Thomas.*

The next was a case of assault, in which one Hannah Rodda was
complainant, and one Mary Edwards defendant.

On being called on, the defendant entered the box and seemed so
devoured with adoration of her own precious self, that she had not a
single glance to spare for any other mortal – and in evidence it appeared
that she had for some time been labouring under a delusion that some
one of her neighbours, had, as she termed it, "ill wished her" that in one
of her enthusiastic mazes of mistaken piety she had conversed with a
supernatural Agent, from whom she learned that nothing short of a sight
of the blood of her who had "ill wished her" could effect a cure-but
unfortunately she had forgotten to enquire the name and residence of her
mystic adversary, and as "Angels" visits are few and far between she sought
the well-known Mrs. Thomas, of Helston[40], who confirmed the supposed
divine revelation, and named the identical person; the secret was

---

[40] This could well be Tammy Blee. Given that by this time Tammy had married James
(Jimmy) Thomas, some may have known her as Mrs Thomas (cf Semmens, 2004)

proclaimed throughout the village, and for some time the complainant evaded the defendant's grasp, but unfortunately on the 3rd inst., after lying in secret for some time, the defendant seized the complainant, and after a severe struggle, succeeded with some instrument in effecting her object, and thus as she exclaimed "found Balm in Gilead," and for which she paid the moderate sum of 1l. 11s. 6d.

Warne was a witch, Falmouth (1845)[41]

West Briton 25.7.1845

FALMOUTH POLICE .- On Tuesday se'nnight[42], three women, named De Freez, were summoned to appear at the Town Hall, on a charge of assault on a woman named Warne. Warne, it appeared, had given some provocation, and a scuffle ensued, in which Warne was severely handled. It came out in examination, that the women charged with the assault could have exonerated themselves, but the neighbours who witnessed the fray were deterred from appearing as witnesses, from the belief that Warne was a witch, and would "ill wish them"!!

---

[41] This incident is mentioned in Deane and Shaw (1975) and Jones (2015).

[42] Meaning seven nights, or a week, ago

White witch of Camborne (1846)

ANN TREBILCOCK, a young girl, was charged with having stolen at St. Columb Minor, a sovereign, the property of Mary Randle.- The prosecutrix was an elderly widow, living at Quintril Downs, with her son and daughter. On the 12th of May, the prisoner being unwell, remained in the house of prosecutrix several hours, during which time prosecutrix was out of the house for some 10 or 12 minutes...

....One of the reasons for the delay in making application to the constable was the strange one that the prosecutrix appeared to have intended to apply to the "white witch of Camborne"- a successor, we presume, of the once-famed conjuror, Johnny Hooper.

A determined attack, Fowey (1846)

RCG 4.12.1846

SUPERSTITION IN THE NINETEENTH CENTURY.-
A landlady who lives not a mile from Fowey, has a son, about 12 years of age, very ill with an affection of the heart, so ill that the advice of eminent medical gentlemen was provided.

Their prescriptions however, not in twenty-four hours fully realising the mother's expectations, she made a determined attack upon a poor weak old woman, who lives a few doors from her in the village, with a large stocking needle, and rent the vein on the back of her right hand, which caused her victim to faint from loss of blood, under the superstitious and foolish idea that her son was bewitched, and that by thus acting, she would remove the spell.

Mark of the Conjuror, Hayle (1846)

RCG 6.2.1846

HAYLE.-The superstitious thieves who robbed the house of Mr. Gregory, at Copper House, as reported in The Gazette last week, were so frightened by the threats of having a conspicuous mark placed in their foreheads by the conjuror, that the whole of the money as found on the following morning thrust under the door which they had broken open the day previously.

Matilda Worten 'The Gipsey Trick', Sithney (1847)

MATILDA WORTEN, 43, was indicted for stealing, from the dwelling-house of Francis Pascoe, in the parish of Sithney, a five pound note and one sovereign, the property of Francis Pascoe. This was one of those gipsey tricks by which poor credulous people are sometimes deceived, and in the end pay for being duped by being robbed of their money. We gave the whole circumstances of the case some weeks since, and therefore need not again relate them in detail.—*Mary Pascoe*, the

West Briton 8.1.1847

MATILDA WORTEN, 43, was indicted for stealing, from the dwelling-house of Francis Pascoe, in the parish of Sithney, a five pound note and one sovereign, the property of Francis Pascoe. This was one of those gipsey tricks by which poor credulous people are sometimes deceived, and in the end pay for being duped by being robbed of their money...

....*Mary Pascoe*, the wife of Francis Pascoe, a miner in Wheal Rose, was in her house at Sithney, on the 9th of last November, when a gipsey (who gives her name Matilda Worten) came in, lighted her pipe, and offered to repeat a few words for the good of Mrs. Pascoe and her family. There was a danger, the gipsey said, hanging over her, she was "ill-wished," and before the 20th of that month her husband or child would be brought home with a leg or an arm smashed unless it were prevented.

Mrs. Pascoe's feelings being wrought upon, she went with the gipsey into another room, where the latter asked for money, as she could do no good to her husband without seeing the money her husband had earned. Ten pounds were asked for, but Mrs. Pascoe could only raise six- a five pound note and a sovereign, which were placed on a mystical book, and afterwards securely tied up by the gipsey, who said she would come again next day. She did so, and untied the parcel, using dreadful words that were "not English," and afterwards she put Mrs. Pascoe upon oath-"*So help me God through salvation, I'll not open this parcel till I sees your face again.*" Mrs. Pascoe afterwards put the money under lock, which the gipsey did not seem to approve of, but she came again the next morning.

In the interim Mrs. Pascoe's daughter had opened the packet, and seen that the money was all there. On coming in the evening the gipsey talked to Mrs. Pascoe's husband, and afterwards getting the packet from Mrs. Pascoe, she again made her take the oath, and then go on her knees to repeat the Lord's prayer with her back towards her. When Mrs. Pascoe arose, the packet was again delivered to her, and she was told not to open it for six days; the gipsey said "then I hope your wants will be satisfied, and you can give me half-a-crown, if not five shillings, and a cup of tea." About half-an-hour afterwards Mrs. Pascoe's eldest daughter opened the parcel, and said "O mother, there's nothing here but a half- penny and a bit of brown paper!"

The constable was then fetched, and chase given to the gipsey, who was found with some of the rest of her tribe, two or three days after in a tent at Probus, twenty-seven miles distant.

She was found GUILTY.

Chicken sacrifice in Bodmin (1848)

RCG 7.7.1848

THE NINETEENTH CENTURY. -To most persons the fact we are about to relate may seem almost incredible but we can offer our assurance of its veracity.-

A respectable farmer in the parish of Bodmin, believing that some ailment of his cattle was the consequence of their being bewitched, has recently attempted as a remedy, the expedient of killing a chicken, and roasting its heart after sticking it over with pins!!!

The experiment has been so recently adopted, that the enlightened agriculturist is still waiting the result. Meanwhile, we understand he is in doubt as to the proper side - right or left - on which, for his own immunity and the health of his cattle, he ought to pass on meeting the supposed witch.

Fishing boats, Padstow (1848)

West Briton 1.12.1848

SUPERSTITION. -Within the last few weeks, the fishing boats of Padstow have caught several thousands of herrings, but one boat being more unfortunate than the others, some persons persuaded the crew that the boat was bewitched.

They then determined to break the charm by nailing a horse shoe to the bottom of the boat, which they did, and the next night caught 1,400 fish, which confirmed the belief that the boat had been bewitched!

Mary Vincent, fortune teller, West Looe (1849)

FAITH IN FORTUNE TELLERS.—At West Looe, on Thursday last, a woman named Mary Vincent, died at an advanced age. This woman had for a great many years carried on a very lucrative business in that town, in "telling fortunes." Great numbers have been in the habit of applying to this impostor, believing she could tell their future destinies, and also to get rid of supposed witchcraft. On the day the old woman died, two young ladies from the neighbourhood of Fowey, called at her house to have their fortunes told; and on the following day, two well dressed middle aged females, from the neighbourhood of Herodsfoot, called to have advice relative to a bewitching case. Both parties left the house sadly disappointed, on finding they were too late.

RCG 23.3.1849

FAITH IN FORTUNE TELLERS. - At West Looe, on Thursday last, a woman named Mary Vincent, died at an advanced age[43]. This woman had for a great many years carried on a very lucrative business in that town, in "telling fortunes." Great numbers have been in the habit of applying to this impostor, believing she could tell their future destinies, and also to get rid of supposed witchcraft.

On the day the old woman died, two young ladies from the neighbourhood of Fowey, called at her house to have their fortunes told; and on the following day, two well-dressed middle aged females, from the neighbourhood of Herodsfoot, called to have advice relative to a bewitching case. Both parties left the house sadly disappointed; on finding they were too late.

---

[43] Parish records for Talland indicate Vincent was 65 when she died.

The Evil Eye, Lifton (1851)

Western Courier 19.3.1851

THE EVIL EYE. – This superstition is still prevalent in this
neighbourhood (Launceston). I have very recently been informed of the
case of a young woman in the village of Lifton who is lying hopelessly ill of
consumption[44] which her neighbours attribute to her having been
"overlooked" (this is the local phrase by which they designate the baleful
spell of the evil eye).

An old woman in this town is supposed to have power of "ill wishing," or
bewitching her neighbours and their cattle, and is looked on with much
awe in consequence. – 'From *Notes and Queries*'

---

[44] Tuberculosis was known as consumption because of the weight loss it tended to cause.

Ann Greenslade, Redruth (1853)[45]

14.1.1853 RCG

PRETENDED WITCHCRAFT AND SORCERY. - ANN GREENSLADE,
44, was indicted for this offence under an ancient statute...

The first count in the indictment stated that Ann Greenslade, the wife of
George Greenslade, on the 9th of October, 1852, at Redruth, unlawfully
and knowingly did falsely pretend to Mary Ann Andrew, wife of Matthias
Andrew, (then confined in the Lunatic Asylum at Bodmin), that the said
Matthias Andrew was ill-wished by two witches, and that she the said Ann
Greenslade had power to conquer and overcome such two witches, and
that thereby the said Matthias Andrew would be cured of the malady
under which he was then labouring, by which said false pretences, the said
Ann Greenslade did obtain from the said Mary Ann Andrew certain
money with intent to defraud the said Ann Greenslade, well knowing the
said pretences to be false...

...To this indictment the prisoner pleaded GUILTY.

---

[45] The census of 1851 shows Ann Greenslade (b1809) living at 37, Buller's Road. In 1855
she served a 4 month sentence for stealing. Parish records show that George Greenslade,
her husband, was a copper miner and that they had three young children living with them.
In 1861 they moved to 32, Foundry Row.

A Gipsy Trick, St Columb Major (1853)

Pigeons.—Black blers, Nuns, Fan-, Truro; Turbots, obins, Mr. T. H. oble, Falmouth.

rcн.—This plough-garton, on Wednes-. were free for the pood, especially the ig won by a "tim-ere were two iron wers awarded as lze, Richard Golly, lds, Cuby; third, le ploughing, first l, Richard Golly, Creed. The prizes eing match, which a the prizes were as ard Golly, Gorran; a; third, William

navvy living in the neighbourhood of Bodmin.

A GIPSY TRICK.—A man of the name of Kessel, living at Trevarren Green, St. Columb Major, was last week swindled by a gipsy woman out of the sum of £30. The particulars of the case are as follows:— For the last few months Kessel and his wife had been both ill, or imagined themselves to have an ailing sickness; one son was also ill, and another son had the misfortune to have his leg broken whilst wrestling, &c. These afflictions, together with the persuasion of a fortune-teller, led them to believe that they were "bewitched" or "ill-wished." The old gipsy also foretold that they would have a succession of misfortunes, and that three sudden deaths would happen in the family. She persuaded Kessel that if he would place £30 in her hands, tied in a parcel, in a peculiar way (the money to be returned to him again) the spell would be broken and overflowing good luck would follow. The poor man could only rise £14 odd, and five shillings he paid the gipsy for a bottle of mixture. The day following his wife borrowed £16 of her neighbours to

A GIPSY TRICK - A man of the name of Kessel, living at Trevarren Green, St. Columb Major, was last week swindled by a gipsy woman out of the sum of £30. The particulars of the case are as follows:- For the last few months Kessel and his wife had been both ill, or imagined themselves to have an ailing sickness; one son was also ill, and another son had the misfortune to have his leg broken whilst wrestling, &c.

These afflictions, together with the persuasion of a fortune-teller, led them to believe that they were "bewitched" or "ill-wished." The old gipsy also foretold that they would have a succession of misfortunes, and that three sudden deaths would happen in the family. She persuaded Kessel that if he would place £30 in her hands, tied in a parcel, in a peculiar way (the money to be returned to him again) the spell would be broken and overflowing good luck would follow.

The poor man could only rise £14 odd, and five shillings he paid the gipsy for a bottle of mixture. The day following his wife borrowed £16 of her neighbours to complete the desired sum, and as he said to prevent death. The gipsy encampment was about a mile from the house. Kessel carried the money tied in a parcel to the gipsy woman three separate times, and which was as regularly returned to him again. The fourth time he carried the money to the encampment was on Tuesday the 26th ult[46]., at nine o'clock in the evening. He gave the parcel to the gipsy, and by her direction knelt on one knee and read the 61st psalm, whilst she on both knees prayed over the money looking at the planets.

A parcel was given to him again, which he believed to be the same, and he swore on the bible not to open it until the Thursday following at twelve o'clock at noon, the woman promising to call at his house at that day and hour when the charm would be complete, and she would then give his wife directions how to take the bottle of mixture. Kessel returned home and went to bed, but not to sleep; reflection came, and he wished to open the parcel, but he had taken an oath not to do so. His wife at length got out of bed and opened it, when he found himself minus £30 with a few bits of brass, &c., in its stead. The policeman and constables were on the alert, but the encampment was broken up, the parties dispersed, and no trace of the fugitive gipsy woman has as yet been found.

The 'paupers' of St Austell (1854)

...nose turning towards the right cheek, and of flushed complexion.

SUPERSTITION.—On Monday last, as the out paupers at St. Austell, were waiting for their relief, a person by the name of Elizabeth Menier, a widow woman, attacked an old woman called Coombe, and scratched the old woman's face so as to cause the blood to flow freely. It appears that Menier had a cow ill some time since, when she consulted a person in Plymouth, called " the White Witch ;" and she told her a person named Ann had bewitched her. She at once fixed on the old woman above-mentioned, as the one, and on Monday having met her, assailed her as described.

DARING ROBBERY AT WEST LOOE.—On Sunday evening last, at the house of Mr. T. Chorth, grocer, while the family was at meeting a robber ...

RCG 10.2.1854

SUPERSTITION – On Monday last, as the out paupers at St. Austell were waiting for their relief, a person by the name of Elizabeth Menier, a widow woman, attacked an old woman called Coombe, and scratched the old woman's face so as to cause the blood to flow freely.

It appears that Menier had a cow ill some time since, when she consulted a person in Plymouth, called "the White Witch;" and she told her a person named Ann had bewitched her. She at once fixed on the old woman above-mentioned, as the one, and on Monday having met her, assailed her as described.

Mary Carter, Fortune Teller, St Cleer (1856)

St. Cleer.—On Saturday last, Mary Carter, a fortune teller, was apprehended by Mr. Santan, constable, for plying her vocation in this village. She first told the fortune of Elfrida Walkey, a young woman, on Thursday, at the low charge of 3d. Learning from Walkey that she had a father in Bodmin Infirmary, Carter said he was illwished, and that she could bring him back again. The mother of Walkey was then called in, and Carter said she could do the husband good, on being paid a 1s., which was at once given her. The fortune teller then produced a book, which she said Mrs. Walkey must cross with gold. A sovereign was brought and afterwards twelve more. This gold was placed on the book and they both crossed it. Carter then wrapped up the gold, and Mrs. Walkey was to lock

RCG 11.4.1856

ST. CLEER – On Saturday last, Mary Carter, a fortune teller, was apprehended by Mr. Santan, constable, for plying her vocation in this village.

She first told the fortune of Elfrida Walkey, a young woman, on Thursday, at the low charge of 3d.. Learning from Walkey that she had a father in Bodmin Infirmary, Carter said he was illwished, and that she could bring him back again. The mother of Walkey was then called in, and Carter said she could do the husband good, on being paid a 1s., which was at once given her. The fortune teller then produced a book, which she said Mrs. Walkey must cross with gold. A sovereign was brought and afterwards twelve more. This gold was placed on the book and they both crossed it.

Carter then wrapped up the gold, and Mrs. Walkey was to lock it away until Saturday when Carter was to call again to see how the spell worked. In the mean time Walkey's fears for her sovereigns being excited, she took them out of the paper and exchanged them for shillings which the fortune teller to her surprise found there on Saturday. The constable dropped in just afterwards and put an end to the charm by taking Carter into custody.

She was at once taken to Liskeard, and brought before a magistrate and committed to the house of correction for one month as a rogue and vagabond.

Mine Robbery (1857)

away the
lly water-
Channel.
attempt-
heavy sea
e keel out
shrouds,
hed from
he masts
vessel be-
eing then
steamer
a flag of
hem, and
e "Jane"
rith can-
ed to be
essel into

GWITHIAN.—A piece of red pine which was recently picked up near this place, has been sold by the Receiver of Droits for the sum of £1 0s. 3d.

MINE ROBBERY.—A robbery took place last week at Wheal Margaret mine, in the parish of Lelant. A man called Samuel Hall, a miner working at the mine, left his watch in the engine house whilst he went underground. When he came up he found his watch gone and could get no intelligence of it; but he thought it possible that a man called Henry Daniel, a miner of St. Ives, who had been working at the mine and who left the day after, might have taken it. He was advised to go to Helston to the conjuror, but hearing that the old lady had departed this life, and that Armitage of the W.C.R. held an apprehending warrant against the husband who had left this part of the county, he applied to the officer himself. When questioned as to whether he had mentioned his suspicions to any one, he said he had. After some further communication St. Ives was visited; and the house where Daniel boarded searched, but no watch was

A purser
Molison,
1834. 15s.
for payme
effected, b
Mr. Hoc1
shores.—(
    NORT\
Mine.—T
Mr. Benja
structive
for plainti
for defend
    KEY c
ditor's pe
said his H
strain the
had been

RCG 13.2.1857

This short article is most likely refers to Tamsin Blee (Thomasine Blight). She was based in Helston from 1841 but died in 1856, and at the time of her death she was living and consulting at 56, Coinagehall Street.

MINE ROBBERY. - A robbery took place last week at Wheal Margaret mine, in the parish of Lelant. A man called Samuel Hall, a miner working at the mine, left his watch in the engine house whilst he went underground. When he came up he found his watch gone and could get no intelligence of it; but he thought it possible that a man called Henry Daniel, miner of St. Ives, who had been working at the mine and who left the day after, might have taken it.

He was advised to go to Helston to the conjuror, but hearing that the old lady had departed this life, and that Armitage of the W.C.R. held an apprehending warrant against the husband who had left this part of the county, he applied to the officer himself.

Belief in Witchcraft, Liskeard (1857)

West Briton 30.1.1857

An article printed a few years later (see West Briton 11.12.1863) suggests that Jimmy Thomas separated from Tammy Blee in 1851 and left West Cornwall for 'upwards of two years'. This article from 1857 may well therefore refer to him.

BELIEF IN WITCHCRAFT.-A correspondent writing from Liskeard under the name of "Philanthropist," says he can vouch for the truth of the following.

A respectable family adjoining the town of Liskeard having lately lost several pigs, attributed the cause of their misfortune to having been "ill-wished." They accordingly sent for a man who professes to be gifted with a supernatural power, to exercise his agency for them, to keep the "evil eye" off their cattle. This man is now a resident of the poor deluded family, for the avowed purpose of giving a counter-charm for the curse which they suppose is now resting on them.

Many other persons in the neighbourhood pay a yearly tribute to the same man for exercising a "beneficent" influence on them. This same person was forcibly expelled from Redruth, and other parts of the county for his imposition on poor deluded creatures who are simple enough to put credence in what he professes.

The writer remarks, it is surprising that persons of a respectable station in life, who have received a good education and live in the nineteenth century, should so hold themselves up to the ridicule of their neighbours by professing belief in an ignorant superstition.

Knowing the man referred to, to be an impostor, (which all are who profess to be gifted with supernatural power), he trusts the deluded people who believe in his arts may after reading this be influenced to abandon principles which are fitted only for the "dark ages."

Elizabeth Williams, Padstow (1860)

and during which it was
r. Kendall, that the actual
850 during the last year.
unty was greatly indebted
ittee, for the time and at-
r of their duties.

the CHAIRMAN suggested
at a committee to confer
rious to the Epiphany Ses-
hen be prepared to decide
roners, in accordance with
rliament to which he had

's suggestion, Sir COLMAN
it of a committee, consist-
Rodd, Mr. Kendall, Mr.
nan, with power to add to
roners that day, after the
motion was agreed to.

VAL DIVISIONS.

committee on this subject
the notice "to receive and
rates of the several petty
heir views, as to the most
present petty sessional di-
just received the reports
committee together to con-
or adjournment was agreed

NCES.

for the further considera-
nan Rashleigh, Bart., that
neral superintendence and

tion of identity, and the jury found a verdict of NOT GUILTY.

FORTUNE TELLING.

ELIZABETH WILLIAMS, 22, charged with stealing a sovereign, from Maria French at Padstow, on the 14th of September.—Mr. Childs conducted the prosecution ; Mr. Cox the defence.—*Maria French*, the prosecutrix, deposed :—I live at Padstow. On the 13th of September the prisoner came to my house and said she would tell my fortune. I said I was too old for that. She then said, I suppose you would not like your husband to be brought home to you a cripple and a bed-lyer. She also said, you have not enjoyed good health of late, have you ? I said, no I have not. She said there is a person who has got power over you ; you are ill wished. I gave her threepence that day. Next day she came again, sat down on a chair at the end of my table, and asked me if I had any rags : I said no ; She went on as before about my husband being brought home a cripple and my being ill-wished, and then she asked me if I had a Bible, and I got her my Bible. She then asked for a piece of newspaper and some coppers ; I gave her a piece of newspaper, and told her I had no coppers. She said haven't you got a halfpenny ? I said yes, but I can't spare it, because it is one I borrowed. Then she said, 'give me a metal button.' I had no metal button, and I gave her a bone one. Then she said 'fetch me a piece of gold to put on it ;' and I fetched a sovereign from upstairs ; I held the sovereign between my finger and thumb, and walked forth to her and said '.I hope you are not going to take away my money from me.' She said, No, I am not going to take away your money ; I am going to do you good ; here is the Bible—God's own Word, and He sees what we are doing. (Sensation in Court.) She requested me to place the sovereign on my left hand ; she then put her hand on mine and began to move about the sovereign, and to tell about the elements and the stars and different things. She then took the sovereign out of my hand and desired me to turn my back a few minutes, and to close the door. I did so, and went out into the passage, and

the opinion of the Coroners on suc...
COUNTY FINANCE.—Sir COLM..
the following gentlemen be app
County Finance :—The three Cha
the four County Members ; Mr. T..
Gully Bennet ; Mr. Glencross ; J..
litho ; Dr. Smith ; Rev. C. M. E..
G. Lakes ; three to form a quorum
nem. con.

Mr. SAWLE seconded the moti...

After discharge of the Petty J...
tence on the prisoners as follows :—
John Roberts, Two Months' hard
Mary Ann Tabb, Three Months' ha
Joseph Johns, Three Months' hard
John Hoare, Four Months' hard la
Elizabeth Ann Maunell, Six Month
Sarah Cornish, Six Months' hard
vant ; and One Month hard la
felony.

Louisa Eade, Twelve Months' hard
Elizabeth Williams, Three Years'
Mary Ann Richard, Four Months'
John Darch, Four Months' hard lal
William Berry, Twelve Months' ha

The group of female prisoners—
Williams, but Maunell less so than
ingly ill-behaved and impudent to
in the dock, and as they received
named seemed to be incited by the
of the fortune-teller Williams.
sentence, made use of an offensive
hoped the Chairman would sit th
Williams was still more impudent
have already stated, she used violen

RCG 19.10.1860

FORTUNE TELLING.

ELIZABETH WILLIAMS, 22, charged with stealing a sovereign, from Maria French at Padstow, on the 14th of September.–

…Maria French, the prosecutrix, deposed:- I live at Padstow. On the 13th of September the prisoner came to my house and said she would tell my fortune. I said I was too old for that. She then said, 'I suppose you would not like your husband to be brought home to you a cripple and a bed-lyer'. She also said, 'you have not enjoyed good health of late, have you?' I said, 'no I have not'. She said 'there is a person who has got power over you; you are ill wished'. I gave her threepence that day.

Next day she came again, sat down on a chair at the end of my table, and asked me if I had any rags: I said 'no'. She went on as before about my husband being brought home a cripple and my being ill-wished, and then she asked me if I had a Bible, and I got her my Bible.

75

She then asked for a piece of newspaper and some coppers; I gave her a piece of newspaper, and told her I had no coppers. She said 'haven't you got a halfpenny?' I said 'yes, but I can't spare it, because it is one I borrowed'. Then she said, 'give me a metal button'. I had no metal button, and I gave her a bone one. Then she said 'fetch me a piece of gold to put on it;' and I fetched a sovereign from upstairs; I held the sovereign between my finger and thumb, and walked forth to her and said 'I hope you are not going to take away my money from me.' She said, 'No, I am not going to take away your money; I am going to do you good; here is the Bible- God's own Word, and He sees what we are doing'. (Sensation in Court.)

She requested me to place the sovereign on my left hand; she then put her hand on mine and began to move about the sovereign, and to tell about the elements and the stars and different things. She then took the sovereign out of my hand and desired me to turn my back a few minutes, and to close the door. I did so, and went out into the passage, and she remained in the kitchen with the sovereign in her hand. When she asked me to turn my back and shut the door, she said 'we don't let everybody see all we do.' Not many minutes afterwards, she opened the door and I returned into the room. She then had in her hand a paper parcel, which she gave to me and said 'here's your money all right, let it remain in your pocket nine days.' I said I could not do without my money so long as that. She then said 'let it remain till to- morrow, and I will call again, but don't look at it, nor tell anybody what has been done' and said, 'for if you do there will be no virtue in it'. She then left the house, and in about a quarter of an hour afterwards I took out of my pocket the parcel she had given me, and found that she had taken the sovereign and left nothing but the button....

...A previous conviction was proved against her...She (Williams) was sentenced to *Three years penal servitude*. On receiving her sentence she behaved most impudently and violently...

'The ill-wish fell on the cat', Liskeard (1863)

West Briton 20.2.1863

The following brief account later appeared, verbatim, in Hunt's 1865 'Popular Romances of the West of England'[47]:

LISKEARD POLICE. – Harriet King was charged with assaulting Elizabeth Wellington. The complainant had called the mother of defendant a witch, and said she had ill-wished a person, and the ill-wish fell on the cat, and the cat died.

This annoyed the daughter, who retaliated by bad words and blows. For the assault, the magistrates fined the defendant 1s. and the costs, £1 in all.

---

[47] Hunt took the text from the Western Morning News. The event is also mentioned in Paynter's 'Cornish Witchcraft'.

Jimmy Thomas of Illogan (1863)

West Briton 27.11.1863

James (or Jimmy) Thomas married Tammy Blight (or Blee) on 10th December 1835. He was 21 years her junior and they worked together as conjurors in both Redruth and Helston, before separating in 1851. Tammy died in 1856. The next three articles, discussing the later exploits of James Thomas, appeared within 6 weeks of each other. The first two (dated 27.11.1863 & 11.12.1863) were reprinted in Hunt's 'Popular Romances' (1865).

GROSS SUPERSTITION.- During the week ending Sunday last, a "wise man" from Illogan, has been engaged with about half-a-dozen witchcraft cases, one a young tradesmen, and another a sea captain. It appears that the "wise man" was in the first place visited at his home by these deluded people at different times, and he declared the whole of them to be spell-bound. In one case he said that if the person had not come so soon, in about a fortnight he would have been in the asylum; another would have had his leg broken; and in every case something very direful would have happened. Numerous incantations have been performed. In the case of a captain of a vessel, a visit was paid to the sea side, and while the "wise man" uttered some unintelligible gibberish, the captain had to throw a stone into the sea. So heavy was the spell under which he laboured, and which immediately fell upon the "wise man," that the latter pretended that he could scarcely walk back to Hayle.

The most abominable part of the incantations is performed during the hours of midnight, and for that purpose the wretch sleeps with his victims, and for five nights following he had five different bed-fellows. Having, no doubt, reaped a pretty good harvest during the week, he returned to his home on Monday; but such was the pretended effect produced by the different spells and witch- craft that fell upon him from his many dupes, that two of the young men who had been under his charge were obliged to obtain a horse and cart and carry him to the Hayle station. One of the men, having had two spells resting on him, the "wise man" was obliged to sleep with him on Saturday and Sunday nights, having spent the whole of the Sunday in his diabolical work. It is time that the police, or some other higher authorities, should take the matter up, as the person alluded to is well known, and frequently visited by the ignorant and superstitious.

West Briton 11.12.1863

This article, which unlike the first, names James Thomas, implies that Tammy and James split up because of James' extra-marital sexual activities.

THE CASE OF GROSS SUPERSTITION AT HAYLE. – In the West Briton of the 27th ult. We gave some particulars of several cases of disgraceful fraud and delusion which had been practised by a pretended

"wise man" from Illogan, and of gross superstition and gullibility on the part of his dupes. A correspondent has furnished us with the following particulars relative to the antecedents of the pretended conjuror.
He states that James Thomas, the conjuror from the parish of Illogan, married some time since the late celebrated Tammy Blee, of Redruth, who afterwards removed to Helston and carried on as a fortune teller, but parted from her husband, James Thomas, on account of a warrant for his apprehension having been issued against him by the magistrates of St. Ives, for attempting to take spell from Mrs. Paynter, through her husband, William Paynter, who stated before the magistrates that he wanted to commit a disgraceful offence[48].

Thomas then absconded, and was absent from the west of Cornwall for upwards of two years. His wife then stated that the virtue was in her and not in him; that she was of the real Pillow[49] blood; and that he could tell nothing but through her. His greatest dupes have been at St. Just and Hayle, and other parts of the West of Cornwall. He has been in the habit of receiving money annually for keeping witchcraft from vessels sailing out of Hayle. He slept with several of his dupes recently; and about a fortnight since he stated that he must sleep with certain young men at Copper-house, Hayle, in order to protect them from something that was hanging over them, one of them being a mason and another miner, the two latter lately from St. Just.

He said himself this week at Truro that he had cured young man of St. Erth, and was going on Saturday again to take a spell from the father, a tin smelter. He has caused a great disturbance amongst the neighbours by charging some with having bewitched others.

He is a drunken, disgraceful, beastly fellow, and ought to be sent to the treadmill. One of the young men is now thoroughly ashamed of himself to think he has been duped so by this scoundrel. We have purposely withheld the names of a number of Thomas's egregious dupes, with which our correspondent has furnished us, believing that the badgering which

---

[48] This may have been some form of same sex intimacy; however Thomas seems to have slept with many other clients without there being an issue (see entries for 1873 & 1874).
[49] This amusing typo was corrected by Hunt (1865). It should read 'pellar'.

they have doubtless received from their friends has proved a sufficient punishment to them, and that their eyes are now thoroughly opened to the gross and disgraceful imposture that has been practised upon them.

A Conjuror.
To the EDITOR of the WEST BRITON.

SIR,—The celebrated conjuror, Jimmy Thomas, of Illogan, (or anywhere else to suit his purpose,) is acquiring through the *West Briton* a degree of notoriety which should make villainy blush, open the eyes of the credulous, and guard the unsuspecting. We are unfortunately familiarly acquainted with him in the beautiful district of Roseland, where he practices his profession with a good degree of success; for he has many disciples here, who, trusting in him more than in their God, subscribe to him annually to ward off all evil. And those who neglect to make good their yearly subscription are threatened with Mr. Thomas's withdrawal of his protection, and told that their afflictions will return and increase. Sheep and geese, if cash be scarce, he condescends to receive.

West Briton 1.1.1864

To the EDITOR of the WEST BRITON

SIR,-The celebrated conjuror, Jimmy Thomas, of Illogan, (or anywhere else to suit his purpose,) is acquiring through the West Briton a degree of notoriety which should make villainy blush, open the eyes of the credulous, and guard the unsuspecting. We are unfortunately familiarly acquainted with him in the beautiful district of Roseland[50] where he practices his profession with a good degree of success; for he has many disciples here, who, trusting in him more than in their God, subscribe to him annually to ward off all evil. And those who neglect to make good their yearly subscription are threatened with Mr. Thomas's withdrawal of his protection, and told that their afflictions will return and increase[51].

---

[50] The main town on the Roseland, St Mawes, is 20 miles from Illogan, and at least 4 hours' walk.

[51] See 'Belief in Witchcraft, Liskeard' (1857). The idea that a pellar would renew a client's magical protection every year is also mentioned by Bottrell (1880) in connection with the Helston pellar. See Appendix B.

Sheep and geese, if cash be scare, he condescends to receive[52]. He visits this neighbourhood about once in three months, and is sometimes sent for on special occasions. Some six months since he was so sent for and supported for three weeks at a farm-house, to rid a youth of that farm of an affiliation case, to describe the particulars of which in detail would be too repulsively amusing.

The young man having been summoned to appear at the Ruan Highlanes petty sessions, James was sent for to stave off justice, at the price of virtue and truth. He continued, and lived nobly, because he said he had to-wrestle hard and pray much in a barn during long days of summer heat, without a wink of sleep in the tempting straw. Very fatiguing this, unless the constitution were well kept up. However, the magistrates assembled, and the young man, his friends, and Jimmy with a horse and cart arrived, Jimmy having his carpet bag with books pretendingly of magic, to perform his wonders on the mental powers of the witnesses and bench of magistrates.

One thing in his performance was plucking single hairs from the right side of his head, and biting each in twain, he would cast it with great energy over his left shoulder, with a grin on his crocodile cheek, looking towards the bench, with a carefully suppressed groan or growl, thereby endeavouring to elicit the fullest confidence from his client and friends, who kept close to his elbow, and had been evidently taught to feel the momentous importance of the case.

But lo to the astonishment of all who had faith in Jimmy, the case was lost. Truth triumphed, and in a few hours Jimmy was dismissed, and the faith of the family and of the neighbourhood was much shaken, since which James's susceptibility has kept him aloof, but the West Briton shows me that he is busy establishing a new circuit in the west. One of our leading gentlemen took offence at Jimmy's conduct some years since, and about three years after he died Jimmy has taken pains since to explain to the public that ____ did not live long after he laid his hand upon him.

---

[52] In other words he can be paid 'in kind'.

At a fishing village close by, there had been no pilchards taken for three or four years. Jimmy stated the cause to be the result of an ill-wish, and volunteered his services for the trifling sum of £3 to remove it, else none of the three sean (seine) boats would take any fish for seven years, but proffered services are seldom appreciated, and Jimmy was not employed, yet each season since the boats have been very successful; and Jimmy lost caste so much on account of this and many minor mistakes and his evil conduct, that he was at last ejected from the village with disgrace. But he finds dupes enough to keep his pockets well lined.

He went one day to a village between Philleigh and Tregony, and came back with £2 in about four hours. He is a tall, thin man somewhat stooping, all legs and wings, takes a great deal of snuff, and is near 60 years of age. One of his chief points is to pretend to be very hard of hearing, which he really is not, but people acting upon this thought, talk freely before him, and without restraint.

Jane Lacy, cunning woman of Penryn (1864)

CORNISH SUPERSTITION.

A case which has naturally created much excitement in the neighbourhood of Penryn has just come before the magistrates of that borough. The defendant, Jane Lacy, residing in the parish of Constantine, known for miles around as a 'cunning' woman, and believed by many to possess wondrous powers in the 'dark art,' was summoned on Monday by P.C. White for having, on the 1st of March last, pretended to use subtle device and craft, in order to remove a spell from a Mrs. Joanna Bate, of Penryn, who died on the 21st ult., by which defendant obtained money. — Mr. Jenkins prosecuted, and Mr. Stokes, of Truro, defended.

Miss Bate, daughter of deceased, said when her mother was first taken ill she employed a nurse and also a medical officer. Three doctors had seen her mother and they all agreed that the disease of which she was suffering was a softening of the brain, but the nurse differed from them, and said she believed that Mrs. Bate was under a spell, and after some time introduced her to Mrs. Lacy. The defendant said she must have a lock of her mother's hair and half-a-crown. Defendant then went upstairs and saw her mother, and when defendant came down a few minutes after she said, ' Your mother has a spell on her, but, with the help of God, in five weeks she shall be the woman she

Cornish Telegraph 1864

Although Jane Lacy of Constantine was 'known as a cunning woman for miles around', it is not clear how she used magic to cure, or attempt to cure, Joanna Bate in the months before she died. She did, however, diagnose her with 'being under a spell'. The news story was syndicated far and wide across the country.

A case which has naturally created much excitement in the neighbourhood of Penryn has just come before the magistrates of that borough. The defendant, Jane Lacy, residing in the parish of Constantine, known for miles around as a 'cunning woman'[53], and believed by many to possess wondrous powers in the 'dark art', was summoned on Monday by P.C. White for having, on the 1st of March last, pretended to use subtle device and craft, in order to remove a spell from a Mrs. Joanna Bate, of Penryn, who died on the 21st ult., by which defendant obtained money. Mr. Jenkins prosecuted, and Mr. Stokes, of Truro, defended.

---

[53] The RCG adds that her reputation was purely with the 'lower classes'.

Miss Bate, daughter of deceased, said when her mother was first taken ill she employed a nurse and also a medical officer. Three doctors had seen her mother and they all agreed that the disease of which she was suffering was a softening of the brain, but the nurse differed from them, and said she believed that Mrs. Bate was under a spell, and after some time introduced her to Mrs. Lacy.

The defendant said she must have a lock of her mother's hair and half-a-crown. Defendant then went upstairs and saw her mother, and when defendant came down a few minutes after she said, 'Your mother has a spell on her, but, with the help of God, in five weeks she shall be the woman she was seven years ago'. Witness asked her what she would have to pay her. Defendant said, 2s. 6d. for examination, and that she would have to pay 12s. 6d. for that day, which would include medicine, and when her mother got about again 12s. 6d. more and 3s. 6d. for medicine.

On the following Tuesday defendant came again and charged her 12s. 6d., and brought some medicine to be taken and liniment to rub the patient's legs with, and told witness her mother was getting better. Defendant said at the nurse's house it was wished that Mrs. Bate's arms might fall useless at her side, and that she should be blind, instead of which the spell had fallen on her legs. Altogether £1. 12s. 6d. had been paid to defendant to have the spell removed.

Mrs. Lacy had also described the person who had ill-wished witness's mother, and said it fell on her mother when the planets were crossing the sun or moon, witness was not sure which...

...The magistrates retired, and after a long consultation, sentenced the prisoner to two calendar months' imprisonment, with hard labour[54].

---

[54] Census data shows that Jane Lacey was born in the parish of Kea, 1822, and in 1851 was living with her parents in Mill Lane, Penryn. In 1861 (as Jane Lacy) she was on a farm in Folow, Constantine owned by the Moyle family. Parish records show that she had two daughters born in the 1850s, and at the time was married to Stephen, 'a retired soldier' who was more than a decade older than her.

Amelia Gribble Fortune Teller Killed (1865)

West Briton 25.8.1865

A FORTUNE TELLER KILLED. - On Thursday last, an inquest was held before Mr. J. Carlyon, county coroner, at Mr. Mitchell's Hotel, Redruth, on the body of Amelia Gribble, who had lived with her husband and four children, at the back of the Tunnel stores in that town[55].

The deceased was one of those individuals who gain a livelihood by professing to be able to peep into futurity, and on their "palms being crossed," to tell the silly persons who consult them the fate that awaits them. It appears that gross superstition prevails to a deplorable extent in the neighbourhood, and that she drove a thriving trade, thousands of persons having consulted her, and as many as thirty persons having been known to visit her in one day.

Though she was able to obtain a good deal of money by her nefarious calling, it seems she was not able to keep it, both she and her husband

---

[55] The census of 1861 describes Amelia Gribble as a miner's wife, aged 31 (b1830), living in East Turnpike Road, Redruth.

86

being addicted to drinking, and the two frequently quarrelled. On Friday and Saturday last, they were drinking as usual, and in a quarrel which took place, her lip was cut and her eyes blackened by blows from the husband... she got to the top of the stairs, and being tipsy and excited, fell to the bottom. ..

In the death by violence of the woman Gribble, late of Shute-row, in this town, the ignorant and superstitious of the neighbourhood have lost one of the greatest and most astute operators in the craft. She was in the confidence of many romantic young ladies of position whose education had been ill-regulated or misdirected. Her gains were considerable, and latterly, having learned that she was considered an expert in befooling the weak, her charges rose proportionately; but having an idle and drunken lout to feed and clothe, and find the means for his unmanly and brutal indulgences, she was always in poverty, and finished her career by falling overstairs while in a state of drunkenness.

Mrs. Gribble has many successors, some less scrupulous, others more criminal, and therefore more dangerous, who, for the value of a shilling in any disposable commodity, will "consult the cards" for the half-witted and foolish. In Redruth, the fortune-teller and the street quack doctor are a pest and a nuisance but unfortunately the law at present is unable to deal with either.

Elizabeth Evans, Bissoe (1865)[56]

WEST POWDER PETTY SESSIONS.—These sessions were held in the Town Hall, Truro, on Saturday, before Mr. J. T. H. Peter (chairman), Messrs. W. T. Chappel and R. T. Polwhele. Richard Burrows, of Creegbrawse, was summoned by Elizabeth Evans, of Bissoe Pool, for assaulting her on the 11th of March. Complainant's statement was, that defendant entered her house, caught her by the throat, and brandished a stick over her head, saying, " I'll take your life." Burrows, when asked what he had to say, replied, " I thought the woman was a witch. I think she ill-wished me, and I pretended to give her a scratch. I have heard that if you go and bring blood they can never hurt you any more. I was not well in body or mind ; and she pretends to do witchcraft, and takes money." The Bench remarked on the ignorance of the defendant, and fined him 1s. and costs. James and Mary Hessett, father and daughter were charged with assaulting Elizabeth

West Briton 7.4.1865

WEST POWDER PETTY SESSIONS. - Richard Burrows, of Creegbrawse, was summoned by Elizabeth Evans, of Bissoe Pool, for assaulting her on the 11th of March.

Complainant's statement was, that defendant entered her house, caught her by the throat, and brandished a stick over her head, saying, "I'll take your life." Burrows, when asked what he had to say, replied, "I thought the woman was a witch. I think she ill-wished me, and I pretended to give her a scratch. I have heard that if you go and bring blood they can never hurt you anymore. I was not well in body or mind; and she pretends to do witchcraft, and takes money."

Bench remarked on the ignorance of the defendant, and fined him 1s. and costs.

---

[56] This case is referred to in Jones' *Cornish Witchcraft* (2015)

88

A Pierced Bull's Heart (1865)

Cornish Telegraph 21.6.1865

Although very verbose, and written with reference to the two warring families in Romeo and Juliet, the following article seems to describe a true incident. It is also worth noting that the farmer that created the pierced heart was a very influential figure in the community.

Witchcraft or ill-wishing still exists with all its startling absurdities in many places as strongly as ever. I give the following strange incident which occurred only a few weeks ago in a parish not ten miles from Tywardreath...

The Montague of the place whose Christian name was Zachariah, possessed an aged gander which one cold frosty night died. There is nothing out of the common course of events that an old gander having lived the lease of nature had paid his breath to time and mortal custom, but so deemed not Montague. He detected some foul play and immediately charged the wife of his hereditary foe (the Capulet) with having ill-wished his gander's life away. Unfortunately for that fair lady's fame an event had recently occurred which rendered her an object of terror and suspicion to many of her neighbours.

A respectable farmer, a ci-devant[57] local preacher, and still the superintendent of a Dissenting school[58], lost very suddenly a large bullock.

Unable to account for the animal's rapid decease, he attributed it to supernatural agency, and became, like Macbeth, bent to know by the worst means the worst, so at 'The witching hour of night' our friend, having carefully cleansed the bullock's heart, pricked it full of pins and thorns, and then roasted it by an ash-wood fire. Mark what followed. No sooner, so the story goes, had the first pin pierced the heart than Mrs. Capulet started from her slumbers: at the second she gave so terrible a shriek that it entirely murdered sleep in Mrs. Capulet for the remainder of the night; and so powerful, it is said, was the magical link that evidently existed between the bullock's heart and the centre of Mrs. C.'s nervous system, that the insertion of every additional thorn or pin caused screams, so that the whole of the family and two or three of the neighbours rushed into the bedroom.

I much regret my inability of informing those who are interested in witchcraft whether the pins, the thorns, or the roasting, caused most suffering; but from that fatal night Mrs. Capulet was considered by most of the inhabitants a witch or ill-wisher, and the sudden death of the gander following so rapidly that of the bullock, was held to confirm the suspicions of those, who had been more charitably inclined.

Montague therefore, took the opportunity of 'feeding fat his ancient grudge against the rival house,' and, aided by all the members of his family, constantly assailed the poor woman with such opprobrious epithets and violent threats that she was compelled to resort to magisterial aid for of protection. Both parties are Brianites[59]. I ought to state that the roasting of the heart, &c., is sometimes preceded by reading a certain chapter from the Bible, and then the suspected person is supposed to be compelled to appear in propria persona.

---

[57] =Former
[58] Dissenting schools did not conform to Church of England doctrine.
[59] Aka Bryanites, or members of the Bible Christian Church, a Methodist denomination originally founded by William O'Bryan in North Cornwall.

Mother and daughter of St Just (1866)

A REMNANT OF OLDEN DAYS, OR THE POWERS OF A WHITE WITCH.—The Sergeant of Police of Penzance met in one of the streets of that town, at three o'clock on Wednesday morning, exposed to a pitiless rain and drenched to the skin, an old woman of 60 and her daughter of about 20. The latter had a baby in her arms. They seemed weary as well as wet, and this was their tale. They lived at Buryan, six miles West of Penzance, and went to bed early on Tuesday evening. They left the front door on the latch for the later retiring to bed of the old woman's son, who was practising with the volunteer band. A thief came in, and stole some gowns, petticoats, skirts, and boots. In the morning the women sought the aid of the Buryan policeman, but he was away. Having heard of the merits of a 'white witch,' a man who lives at Helston, and who gains a good livelihood by pretended sorceries and divinations, the poor old soul and her daughter, carrying the child, started on foot for Penzance and thence for Helston, very nearly 20 miles. The wizard was from home, and they had returned from Helston to Penzance, and were on their way to Buryan, when the Sergeant saw them and bade them rest awhile. Upon the subject of the robbery, and any other topic, mother and daughter were

Cornish Telegraph 15.8.1866

A REMNANT OF OLDEN DAYS, OR THE POWERS OF A WHITE WITCH.-The Sergeant of Police of Penzance met in one of the streets of that town, at three o'clock on Wednesday morning, exposed to a pitiless rain and drenched to the skin, an old woman of 60 and her daughter of about 20. The latter had a baby in her arms. They seemed weary as well as wet, and this was their tale.

They lived at Buryan, six miles West of Penzance, and went to bed early on Tuesday evening. They left the front door on the latch for the later retiring to bed of the old woman's son, who was practising with the volunteer band. A thief came in, and stole some gowns, petticoats, skirts, and boots. In the morning the women sought the aid of the Buryan policeman, but he was away. Having heard of the merits of a 'white witch', a man who lives at Helston, and who gains a good livelihood by pretended sorceries and divinations, the poor old soul and her daughter, carrying the child, started on foot for Penzance and thence for Helston, very nearly 20 miles. The wizard was from home, and they had returned from Helston to

Penzance, and were on their way to Buryan, when the Sergeant saw them and bade them rest awhile.

Upon the subject of the robbery, and any other topic, mother and daughter were shrewder than the average of our labouring classes, but they had a firm faith in the occult and wondrous power of this white witch, and preferred his abracadabra to the keenness of any detective we have. Having sat a bit, they started for home, and accomplished the 40 miles walk, unsolaced by the conjuror, and making light of it, but for the baby's weight. Early the next day the young mother was in Penzance again, another six miles, but the wizard had been abandoned for a search at pawnshops and other places.

Our Sergeant probably shook this nearly extinct faith in professors of the black art.

Divination by post (1867)

14, Duke-street, Adelphi, London, W.C.

YOUR FUTURE HUSBAND or WIFE'S TRUE CARTE DE VISITE.—Mr. HOWARD the celebrated Astrologer, will send the true Carte de Visite of your Intended, with Name, Age, and Date of Marriage, for Sixteen Stamps. Three Questions answered for 2s. 6d. State age and sex. Send stamped directed envelope. Address Mr. Howard. Victoria Villa, Portland-road, Notting Hill. London. Nativities cast.

Falmouth Packet 2.3.1867

Dolly Pentreath, alias Dolly the Spring (1867)

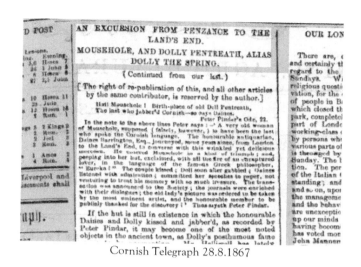

Cornish Telegraph 28.8.1867

Dolly Pentreath, famous as a Cornish language speaker, died in 1777.

Dolly, from her skill in fortune-telling, charming for the cure of various diseases, giving directions to the young folks as to the best way of trying for sweethearts, and other practices of divination, came to be regarded as one of those who have acquired so much forbidden knowledge that they have the power to blast and ban, to lay a spell on man or beast, so that the old dame was little loved, but what is the next best thing, much feared as one of those over-wise ones about whom we now often hear the whisper accompanied by the ominous shake of the head, that she knows the hour and the minute: on that account it is much better not to offend the one who holds the dreaded secret.

This mysterious intimation alludes to the general belief that there is an hour in every day, and a minute, only known to the demon-taught, in that particular hour, in which as we say 'curses will not fall to the ground'. This notion seems to be some vestige of the dogmas belonging to judicial astrology perhaps the shadow of some idea about the culmination of the malignant planet. However that may be, the belief exists to the present hour; also that our pellars (conjurors,) white witches (or by whatever name. these wise people are distinguished) have a profound acquaintance with this mysterious science.

It seems that Dolly was also regarded as one having this knowledge, and more fearful kinds of wisdom, by the stories still told of her. When much excited, she seemed to forget the little English she knew, and her voluble fast and harsh Cornish speech, then imperfectly understood by the younger and educated folks, impressed the people with far greater terrors than if she cursed or scolded in a language of which they knew the import.

Gipsies in Trouble, Penzance (1867)

GIPSIES IN TROUBLE.—Charlotte Cory and Gentilla Small were brought before the Mayor of Penzance, F. Boase, Esq., on Thursday, and charged with fortune-telling. Cory and Small are sisters, and members of a well-known gipsy tribe. Cory is of ruddy complexion and shews no sign of gipsy blood. She has four children and daily expects another; and she will not be soon forgotten in Cornwall, as she was one of the tribe committed to gaol by the Rev. Uriah Tonkin—a proceeding which raised an outcry throughout the country. She told the magistrate that she is the oldest of nine children, and that her husband makes baskets, clothes' pegs, and tin-ware, which she and her sister sell. Gentilla Small is a true and swarthy gipsy. She said she did not know her age, but she thought it was 20. Her married sister said it was 18. Policeman Taylor arrested them under the following circumstances. A little before 10 he saw them in conversation with the servants of Mr. Paddon, draper, just opposite the police office. They soon moved away, and passed up the pork market. Suspicious of their procedure, he followed them in a short time, and found them in a shed in Mrs. Runnalls'

Cornish Telegraph 4.9.1867

94

GIPSIES IN TROUBLE. – Charlotte Cory and Gentilla Small were brought before the Mayor of Penzance, F. Boase, Esq., on Thursday, and charged with fortune-telling. Cory and Small are sisters, and members of a well-known gipsy tribe. Cory is of ruddy complexion and shows no sign of gipsy blood. She has four children and daily expects another; and she will not be soon forgotten in Cornwall, as she was one of the tribe committed to gaol by the Rev. Uriah Tonkin's proceeding which raised an outcry throughout the country.

She told the magistrate that she is the oldest of nine children, and that her husband makes baskets, clothes' pegs, and tin-ware, which she and her sister sell. Gentilla Small is a true and swarthy gipsy. She said she did not know her age, but she thought it was 20. Her married sister said it was 18. Policeman Taylor arrested them under the following circumstances.

A little before 10 he saw them in conversation with the servants of Mr. Paddon, draper, just opposite the police office. They soon moved away, and passed up the pork market. Suspicious of their procedure, he followed them in a short time, and found them in a shed in Mrs. Runnalls' field – the married one talking very intently to the two servants, Gentilla Small with the hand of one of the female shop-assistant's in hers, so deep in the art of palmistry that she could not tell her own fortune (or misfortune,) viz., that she would be locked up in a minute or two. At the sight of the policeman's blue coat and bright buttons the dupes of the foretellers of Fate ran as if old Scratch himself was at their heels, and the gipsies were arrested.

The mayor inquired as to the term of punishment awarded this kind of vagrancy, when both women began to weep, and begged piteously not to be sent to prison, Cory explaining, in answer to a suggestion from the Mayor, that she expected her confinement daily and should not like her child to be born in gaol. If the gentleman would forgive them, they would never tell fortunes in Penzance again.

The Mayor considered some time, and then said he hardly knew which were the most to blame-deceivers like those before him, or their brainless dupes. One thing was certain: the pretence to tell fortunes often caused loss to masters and mistresses, and exercised an influence that was sometimes baneful on the misguided believers in this kind of divination. Cory's condition had saved her from gaol this time, and her sister also, as the latter would soon he wanted as nurse. He warned them, however, never to come before him again.-

Cory: Never again, sir.-

Small: Thank you, my gentleman.

The Mayor: Mind, now: three months is the period you can be sent to gaol for: so sell your wares, but avoid fortune-telling[60].

The Liskeard Devil (1868)

A Singular Case of Superstition has occurred at Liskeard. A "white witch" of that town was consulted by the son of a farmer, supposed to be "ill-wished" by the wife of a labouring man residing on the estate. On the recommendation of the witch the latter was discharged. The "ill-wished" man fell sick, and during the night was visited by the village blacksmith. The latter, on going to the sick man's house one night, saw something like a goat; the next night it assumed the form of the devil. The witch on being consulted ordered that a gun should be kept loaded, charged with fourpenny-pieces broken into

Cornish Echo and Falmouth Times 18.7.1868

A *Singular Case of Superstition* has occurred at Liskeard.

A "white witch" of that town was consulted by the son of a farmer, supposed to be "ill- wished" by the wife of a labouring man residing on the estate. On the recommendation of the witch the latter was discharged.

---

[60] See entry for 1881.

The "ill-wished" man fell sick, and during the night was visited by the village blacksmith. The latter, on going to the sick man's house one night, saw something like a goat; the next night it assumed the form of the devil. The witch on being consulted ordered that a gun should be kept loaded, charged with fourpenny-pieces broken into hand-small bits. The blacksmith kept a strict watch the succeeding night, and fired to the great alarm of the villagers.

It is said that the case is to come before the magistrates.

Superstition and Swindling, Feock (1868)

In 1868 William Rapson Oates was an unscrupulous young cunning man (b1843)[61]. In this case he appears to have stolen some clothes, using a magical operation as a pretext.

SUPERSTITION AND SWINDLING.
William Rapson Oates, 25, herbalist, was indicted for obtaining by false pretences a coat, a pair of trousers, and a silk pocket-handkerchief, the property of George Sara, at Feock, and...disposing of it fraudulently to his own use, and that he thereby did steal the same.

---

[61] See Semmens, 2014.

The prosecutor in this case is a sailor, and on the 20th of August last he was at sea. By some means the prisoner became aware of this fact, and on that day he went to the prosecutor's mother, who is a very old woman, and represented to her that, by having possession of her son's coat and trousers he could ensure his safety from being drowned. He did not require the articles for his own use, but announced his intention of secreting them in some distant churchyard for three successive nights, at the end of which time he promised faithfully to return them.

This he did not do, whereupon information was given to the police, and he was shortly afterwards apprehended. The prisoner's defence was that the articles were given him by the old woman as an acknowledgment of valuable services which he had rendered to her son five years' previously, but this was denied by Mrs. Sara, and the jury found the prisoner guilty.

A previous conviction for a similar offence was proved against the prisoner, who appears to be a noted schemer. Besides the case now proved against him, there might have been another for obtaining money under false pretences. He personated the son of the chief warder of the county prison, and as such obtained much kindness and money assistance from an acquaintance of that officer living at Redruth. He is a man against whom the public ought to be warned, as a heartless scoundrel, who will not stop at anything to swindle and cheat his fellows, either by fraud or lying. He had been discharged as worthless from the Miners' Artillery. He was sentenced to nine months' imprisonment with hard labour.

Epilepsy ring, North Hill (1869)

SUPERSTITION.—On Sunday last, as the Parishioners of North-hill were leaving the neat and recently-restored parish church, a scene of the grossest superstition met their view in the church porch. A young man, who had just been in a fit, was collecting one penny each from 30 unmarried women, for the purpose of purchasing a silver ring, to wear on his finger as a sure preventive against all future attacks from fits. This is the second occurrence of the kind within the last few months, a young woman having collected from 30 young men for the same purpose a month or so since. This conduct was unknown to the rector, or it would, doubtless, have been forbidden.

RCG 18.9.1869

This is a charm known in other parts of the UK, and versions of it appear in Hunt (1865) and Courtney (1890), the latter referring to a case in St Just. The more usual procedure was to make a ring from the silver collected, rather than use the money to buy one, however.

SUPERSTITION. – On Sunday last, as the Parishioners of North-hill were leaving the neat and recently-restored parish church, a scene of the grossest superstition met their view in the church porch. A young man, who had just been in a fit, was collecting one penny each from 30 unmarried women, for the purpose of purchasing a silver ring to wear on his finger as a sure preventative against all future attacks from fits. This is the second occurrence of the kind within the last few months a young woman having collected from 30 young men for the same purpose a month or so since. This conduct was unknown to the rector, or it would, doubtless, have been forbidden.

The following week 25.8.1869 a rather poignant response appeared in the RCG:

AN APOLOGIST FOR SUPERSTITION. – Sir,- There having appeared in your last week's issue, a paragraph under the heading "Superstition," I beg to be allowed space to state the facts of the case of the young woman, whom your correspondent makes mention of, so that the public may know both sides of the case, and choose for themselves which is right for a person to do. To try an experiment of such an easy thing as standing in the church porch and gathering thirty pence from so many young men, or to suffer a lifetime with such a detestable thing as those fits which have now passed away.

Whether your correspondent ever saw any one in fits I cannot say, but this I will say, that if he saw the young woman in fits, that he makes mention of in his remarks, he would have spared himself the trouble and expense of writing about such things. Sir, the facts are these:- About two years ago this young woman was a great sufferer from those fits, and having been persuaded to purchase a silver ring, with the money collected at the church door, as a sure preventive of any future attack, she tried it. What was the result? The fits left, and nothing more was seen of them, until one day, she accidentally wiped the ring off, and the fits came on again with their usual severity, the ring having been on the finger more than twelve months. Now after the ring came off, the fits still increased with such power and rapidity, that she could not be trusted anywhere, and it took four men to hold her, when she would remain in that state for three or four hours at a time. I would ask whether it was right or wrong to try such a simple thing, when the poor creature put faith in it, after the surgeon saying he could do nothing for her.

Your correspondent also states "that the people were annoyed on leaving the neat church at North-hill." I would ask, who were those that were annoyed, by what they pleased to term gross superstition; and also about the rector not allowing such conduct? I believe he would much rather see the young woman at the church door to gather money for another ring than he would see her in such a state as he did about six months ago, while in one of her fits; and if I am rightly informed, he gave his consent for her to get another ring, which was speedily done, the result being as before – no fits or signs of any such thing.

And as to the young man referred to, he has had no fits since he purchased his ring. This being an affliction sent by God, which we are all liable to, I would advise your correspondent never more to try to weaken the faith of the afflicted in such cases as these.- Yours truly, "SYMPATHY & TRUTH."

The Mermaid and the gossips, Cury (1869)

Cornish Telegraph 7.4.1869

The year before his first volume of folklore was published, William Bottrell, using the pen name 'Old Celt', published extracts from his book in The Cornish Telegraph. Here follows the last section of the droll of the mermaid who grants Lutey of Cury magic powers after he saves her:

....on the way home, he (Lutey) related how he found a stranded mermaid; that for taking her out to sea, she had promised to grant his three wishes, and given him the comb (which he showed his wife) as a token; "but," said he, "if it hadn't been for the howling of our dog Venture, to rouse me out of the trance, and make me see how far I was from land, as sure as a gun I should now be with the mermaidens drinkan rum or huntan sharks at the bottom of the sea."

When Lutey had related all particulars, he charged his wife not to say anything about it to the neighbours, as some of them, perhaps, wouldn't credit his strange adventure; but she, unable to rest with such a burden on her mind, as soon as her husband went away to his work, she trotted round half the parish to tell the story, as a great secret, to all the courtseying old women she could find, and showed them what Lutey gave her as the mermaid's comb, to make the story good.

The wonder (always told by the old gossips as a great secret) was talked of far and near in the course of a few weeks, and very soon folks, who were bewitched or otherwise afflicted, came in crowds to be helped by the new pellar or conjuror.

Although Luty had parted from the mermaid in a very ungracious manner, yet he found that she was true to her promise. It was also soon discovered that he was endowed with far more than the ordinary white-witch's skill.

.....Here ends the droll-teller's story.

(That the extraordinary powers, said to have been conferred by the mermaid, have continued with this gifted race, down to the present day, there are hundreds alive to testify among those who yearly consult Tammy Blee and J. Thomas. This worthy couple of white witches seem to be equally successful in the exercise of their art, though many say that the former only is of the true old pellar blood. So strong was the faith in this woman's power, a short time since, that many believed she could raise spirits from their graves....[62]

It is somewhat remarkable that, from a very remote period, the parish of Cury, or its vicinity, has been the head-quarters of persons noted for performing extraordinary cures. There have been various opinions with respect to the derivation of the name of Cury (pron. *Cure*).

---

[62] Regarding 'being of pellar blood' see West Briton 11.12.1863. This account of magical powers being conferred by a mermaid is thought to be unique to Cornwall.

The Black Dog of St Agnes (1871)

WITCHCRAFT AT St. AGNES.

There is a family in St. Agnes, who, having lost their father some time since, pretend to have been troubled with his spirit coming on earth in different forms, sometimes like a great black dog, at other times making noises as if all the clome in the house was breaking to pieces. The family had consulted a man in Illogan parish who pretends to be a wizard. He told them he must sleep three nights in the bed the father died in to put him to rest, and he also said they were ill-wished. One of the nights they had to go to bed and leave him up by a very large fire to put the dead to rest and burn the witch, who is a young woman living in St. Agnes, and who has been corresponding with their son in California for a great many years. Lately, they have written against her and broke off the correspondence, which is supposed to be the reason why they condemn her for ill-wishing them !

The Cornish Telegraph 1.3.1871

The following 'wizard', though not named, is almost certainly Jimmey Thomas.

WITCHCRAFT AT St. AGNES.

There is a family in St. Agnes, who, having lost their father some time since, pretend to have been troubled with his spirit coming on earth in different forms, sometimes like a great black dog, at other times making noises as if all the clome in the house was breaking to pieces.

The family had consulted a man in Illogan parish who pretends to be a wizard. He told them he must sleep three nights in the bed the father died in to put him to rest, and he also said they were ill-wished. One of the nights they had to go to bed and leave him up by a very large fire to put the dead to rest and burn the witch, who is a young woman living in St. Agnes, and who has been corresponding with their son in California for a great many years. Lately, they have written against her and broke off the correspondence, which is supposed to be the reason why they condemn her for ill-wishing them!

Fortune-telling, Falmouth (1873)

Fortune Telling.

At a sitting of the Penryn Borough magistrates, on Saturday last, a case was heard which proves that the boasted ·enlightenment of the century has not yet eradicated the belief in witchcraft. A thin, spare man, who called himself Dr. Thomas, and said he lived at Park Bottom, Illogan, was charged by P.C. Edwards with fortune-telling, &c. The prisoner, on being requested to plead, feigned deafness ; but, as the case went on, he entirely recovered the use of his ears, and said he was the seventh son of a seventh daughter, and cousin to Sir Charles Sawle. He also exhibited a valuable gold watch, which he said was given him by Mrs Plomb, of Colchester, with a harmonium and quilt, for curing her of heart disease. He said he had cured all sorts of diseases all through England to numberless persons. John Collins was called, and, in answer to the Bench, said he was an apprenticed pilot, 20 years of age, and lived in Gilling street, Falmouth. He had

RCG 6.9.1873

Jimmey Thomas was about 60 when this article was published. Less than two years earlier (May 10th 1871) he had appeared in the Cornish Telegraph after being assaulted in his house in Park Bottom, Illogan. His assailants were two young miners who were well known to him and, rather than steal all his savings, were kind enough to leave him some money so he could buy some snuff.

Fortune Telling.

At a sitting of the Penryn Borough magistrates, on Saturday last, a case was heard which proves that the boasted enlightenment of the century has not yet eradicated the belief in witchcraft. A thin, spare man, who called himself Dr. Thomas, and said he lived at Park Bottom, Illogan, was charged by P.C. Edwards with fortune-telling, &c.

The prisoner, on being requested to plead, feigned deafness; but, as the case went on, he entirely recovered the use of his ears, and said he was the seventh son of a seventh daughter, and cousin to Sir Charles Sawle. He also exhibited a valuable gold watch, which he said was given him by Mrs Plomb, of Colchester, with a harmonium and quilt, for curing her of heart disease. He said he had cured all sorts of diseases all through England to numberless persons.

John Collins was called, and, in answer to the Bench, said he was an apprenticed pilot, 20 years of age, and lived in Gilling Street, Falmouth. He had a message from the prisoner desiring him to call at Mrs Hill's refreshment rooms, Penryn. He did so the previous evening, about nine o'clock. He was prepared to receive him, and took him into a room, where he told him his name was John, and that he could see it engraved on his forehead. He was born between two unlucky planets, Mars and Jupiter.

'He told me', continued Collins, 'I was cautioned by a Swedish captain three years ago that I should be drowned'. He said, 'You know a female whose name begins with A, and that person would rather see you drowned than that the young woman you are now keeping company with should have you'. 'He said I was ill-wished by two women. Asked me if I had not been in danger lately, and said it looks to me as if you had been nearly drowned, and you wore saved by a rope with another young man'.

The Town Clerk here asked if there were any grounds for the questions put to witness by the prisoner, and he said most of the things did happen. He was nearly drowned and saved by a rope; and the Swedish captain told him three years before that he would be drowned.

During the time prisoner made these inquiries (the plaintiff continued) he was sitting at a table, writing and muttering. Sometimes shading his eyes as if he was electrified, and said the power was coming, he felt it in his throat. He asked me if I knew a female whose name commenced with A. I said "Yes." He then said you have been on disagreeable terms, but are not now, with a man called James, which was true. He could see three deaths at Falmouth, one man, woman and child. He told me I was near death, and that I should be drowned on the 16th of next month, and that unless I stayed there all night he could not remove the spell.

He said it was almost incurable; I must stay the night and sleep with him. He gave me a piece of paper to wear in a bag around my neck (the paper produced had on it a few marks, and the CHAIRMAN thought he could decipher the word "humbug." under them). The witness slept with

105

prisoner that night, during which he continued to mutter about Mars, a pilot boat, and a punt. In the morning we arose, and the prisoner said he was going away by an early train[63].

I paid him 3s, and also 2s 6d for the use of the consulting room, bed, and refreshment. He said on leaving I was never to be without the bag around my neck, and never to let it touch the ground, or its virtue would be lost. I was never to turn a candle upside down, but to blow it out or put an extinguisher on it.

The prisoner, who insisted he was half proprietor of the Vessel Nelly, of Devoran, and shareholder of all the best mines in Cornwall, was committed to Bodmin County Gaol for one month's hard labour.

Death of a Cornish Wizard (1874)

DEATH OF A CORNISH WIZARD.

James Thomas, of Broadlane, Illogan, known as "Dr Jimmey Thomas, the Wizard," died suddenly at his house on Wednesday morning. It appears that a man named John Odgers, of Camborne, who is unwell, believing himself to be ill wished, consulted Thomas, who told him in order to get the spell removed it would be necessary for him to sleep with him (Thomas). He, therefore, did so. Odgers having risen shortly before eight on Wednesday morning, Thomas requested him to light the fire and get the tea ready for breakfast whilst he (Thomas) dressed himself. Odgers had not been in the kitchen long before he heard a noise in the chamber. On going upstairs, he found Thomas on the floor insensible, and soon afterwards he was a corpse. A correspondent writes :—Death has taken away rather a remarkable member of society—"Jammy

RCG 28.2.1874

---

[63] The railway - still a relative novelty - reached Falmouth in 1863.

Within six months of the fortune-telling incident in Falmouth, Jimmey Thomas was dead. He received surprisingly affectionate send-offs from both of the main papers in Cornwall:

DEATH OF A CORNISH WIZARD.

James Thomas, of Broadlane, Illogan, known as "Dr Jimmey Thomas, the Wizard," died suddenly at his house on Wednesday morning. It appears that a man named John Odgers, of Camborne, who is unwell, believing himself to be ill wished, consulted Thomas, who told him in order to get the spell removed it would be necessary for him to sleep with him (Thomas).

He, therefore, did so. Odgers having risen shortly before eight on Wednesday morning, Thomas requested him to light the fire and get the tea ready for breakfast whilst he (Thomas) dressed himself. Odgers had not been in the kitchen long before he heard a noise in the chamber. On going upstairs, he found Thomas on the floor insensible and soon afterwards he was a corpse.

A correspondent writes:- Death has taken away rather a remarkable member of society- "Jemmy, the Wizard," or, as he liked to be called, "Dr." Thomas. On Wednesday morning he was found upstairs dead on the floor by a young man, who was receiving a "wizardous" treatment for a disease in the feet, for the removal of which, as a preliminary, it appears he had to pass a vigil with the wizard.

"Dr." Thomas, when an ordinary being, married Fanny (sic) Blee, the "witch of Helston," on whose death the mantle was transferred to the widower, together with all its mystical lore[64], and it lacked nothing of its power by transmission, for many a one labouring under a "spell" has had its infernal enchantment removed by him through his deep penetration into the dark mysteries of the evil one, and all future attacks effectually guarded against by his powerful talisman. Not from man alone was the dire effects of an evil wish removed, but the livestock of the farm, which groaned under the curse, again regained their sleek appearance as the evil influence was dispelled by the great magician, while the fascinated farmer,

---

[64] Unlike other accounts to the contrary, this report suggests Thomas did not become a magician until after he met Blee.

for the supposed good done, contributed a yearly sum to avert a future calamity of a like kind[65]. "Dr." Thomas, holding just the same position among a certain class of society as the medicine man of the North American Indians and other savage tribes, is among the fast disappearing race of witches and wizards. Still they have their representatives, perhaps, in the nineteenth century in the "mediums" of the Spiritualists.

West Briton 26.2.1874

JOHN THOMAS, THE WIZARD. - On Thursday last, at Park Bottom, in the parish of Illogan, John Thomas, better known as "the wizard," ended his mortal career somewhat abruptly, and without any apparent warning of its approach. It appears, from particulars received, that John Odgers, a native of Camborne, laboured under the conviction that he was "bewitched," "ill-wished," and otherwise troubled, and to be relieved of the burdens upon his mind he straightway consulted the oracle....

....The defunct wizard in his lifetime clearly studied the weak side of human nature to some purpose, as facts would show if we were permitted to publish much of what we know and more of what we have heard

---

[65] Another reference to having protection renewed on an annual basis (see eg 1864 entry)

concerning his clients. Rich and poor for miles around the wizard's dwelling-place have honoured him with a visit, and the contributions poured in upon him must, if report be true, have been considerable. Every species of ailment which afflicts the human family he was supposed to cure.

If swine were possessed of unnatural propensities, or took to dying in an unceremonious manner, John could tell their owners all about it; or if cows misbehaved themselves, adopted vicious tricks and refused to do the correct thing, the wizard soon brought them to their senses. Among horses he was indeed a host; a kicker might as well be a dead horse, as far as kicking went, after John had worked his will upon him; and as to stopping blood, if an arm was lopped off no blood would flow if John cried stop; while to the poor benighted pig-killer he was a terror-the long keen knife could never hit the vein or artery if the wizard was in time to work the spell. Such are the stories told, and, sad to say, believed by hundreds. Whoever wears the mantle of the wizard, if he be cunning, slow of speech, looks wise, and studies well his part, he will find fools still left to feast upon if he has wit to eat.

The following year he received a much less appreciative acknowledgement from the Cornish Telegraph:

LOCAL WITCHES AND WIZARDS.

I don't know how the trusters in those who "have familiar spirits" will "fadgey," now that those persons are getting so beautifully less. "Tammy the Witch" is long dead, and the old black cat has succumbed to the morbid misery of living alone. Her friends and patrons, for many years, found in "Jimmy the Wizard," alias "doctor," a sincere sympathizer in the weight of their pockets, and he "proved" himself equal to the exigencies of many a serious case. Cows, pigs, horses, men, women, and children suffering from the ill-wishing vengeance of some local spirit of evil, were taken under his care; while his ass-throw-logical and neck-rogue-mau-tic ability were clearly proved by his soothsaying expertness, resulting in impressing his devotees with the notion of his "awful"

Cornish Telegraph 14.7.1875

I don't know how the trusters in those who "have familiar spirits" will "fadgey," now that those persons are getting so beautifully less. "Tammy the Witch" is long dead, and the old black cat has succumbed to the morbid misery of living alone. Her friends and patrons, for many years, found in "Jimmy the Wizard", *alias* "doctor," a sincere sympathizer in the weight of their pockets, and he "proved" himself equal to the exigencies of many a serious case. Cows, pigs, horses, men, women, and children suffering from the ill-wishing vengeance of some local spirit of evil, were taken under his care: while his ass-throw-logical and neck-rogue-man-tic ability were clearly proved by his soothsaying expertness, resulting in impressing his devotees with the notion of his "awful" superiority over the spirits of the "vast deep".

To that vast deep he also has gone, having left his mantle of gloomy "mystery" to the Camborne "Emperor,"[66] around and within whose dwelling weird-like[67] music has, to the midnight hour, broken upon the startled ears of the slumbering ones about. Those screams and yells of witchy-type are hushed in the stillness of the grave, and we are left to wonder upon whom her shade has cast a shadow; and who will come forward to cut the cords, or describe the mystic circle?

---

[66] Reference to fortune teller Ann Emperor (who had possibly already died by then - see 1875 entry).
[67] The print here is difficult to read

Ill-wished brother, Truro (1874)

West Briton 2.7.1874

This day Monday Elizabeth Waters was summoned for assaulting Emily McKay who resides in Charles Street. The prosecutrix stated that she was cleaning some fish at her back door when the defendant came up without any provocation and struck her on the back. When she turned round the defendant struck her in the face and knocked her senseless and her mother and her afterwards pulled her by the hair and struck her. She screamed murder and the neighbours came to her assistance.

The defendant pleaded guilty and stated that the reasons she committed the assault was that some six weeks ago the prosecutrix expressed an ill-wish towards her brother, who had since died. Defendant was fined 10s. 6d. and 14s. 6d. costs.

Richard Couch, Chacewater Rag and Bone Man (1874)

RCG 14.2.1874

SUPERSTITION IN CORNWALL.

The following case heard at the magistrates' clerk's office, Truro, will show that superstition, notwithstanding the increased enlightenment of all classes, is still found in Cornwall. A "rag and bones" man, named Richard Couch, was charged with attempting to commit a rape on Louisa Phillipe, a girl 17 years of age.

For this charge he was committed for trial; but the most remarkable part of the evidence was the superstition of Louisa's sister, Mary Ann Phillips, a full grown woman. She is a servant with the Rev. G. L. Church, Chacewater, and on February 7th, the prisoner called at Mr Church's house to buy rags and bones. He then told her that she was ill-wished, and that he could cure her by Thursday, 10 o'clock, for 2s.

"The man who has ill-wished you," said the prisoner," shall come here by 10 o'clock, and he shall knock at the door and ask how you are, and he shall lose his mouth-speech and the use of his arms until sunset, and I will

112

give you the money back again." I gave him, continued the witness, 2s, and he left. He returned again the following day about eleven o'clock, and he said "There are two wishes put on you, one that you (witness) might lose the use of your arms and legs, and the other that you might die a lingering death." He said he must have another shilling. I gave him a shilling, and he left.

The same afternoon he came again, and seemed to be in a great fright. He said, "I want five minutes with you privately," and I took him into the stable. He said "You have not got more than fourteen minutes more; there is another party working as hard as me against the seventeenth of the month; if you had not seen me you would have been a corpse; you must give me another shilling," and I did so.

He then said, "I have finished with you, I should like to see your sister." The witness fetched her sister, and afterwards gave evidence against the prisoner, having been called to her sister by hearing her scream[68]. Louisa Phillips also gave evidence. When she went to the prisoner, at his request she showed him her arm, and he said her father had been ill-wished and that the curse was following her. The prisoner has been previously convicted.

---

[68] Official court records describe Richard Couch as a 33 year old rag-gatherer, who was accused of 'Unlawfully assaulting one Louisa Phillips, with intent against her will to feloniously ravish and carnally know her'. They also note that he pleaded guilty, and was sentenced to two year's hard labour.

Death of Ann Emperor, Camborne (1875)

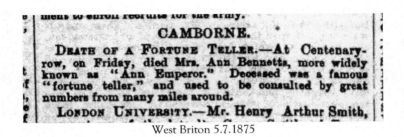

West Briton 5.7.1875

CAMBORNE.

DEATH OF A FORTUNE TELLER - At Centenary row, on Friday, died Mrs. Ann Bennetts, more widely known as "Ann Emperor." Deceased was a famous "fortune teller," and used to be consulted by great numbers from many miles around[69].

---

[69] Only a few months earlier, on 31st March, The Cornish Telegraph had reported: 'Incorrigible Drunkard: Ann Bennetts, fortune-teller, recent before the Penzance magistrates, was in trouble again for being drunk and disorderly'. Indeed three other incidents of 'drunkenness' are reported in the papers, the first dating from 1872, when Ann, aged 60, was 'apprehended (in Camborne) at 2 o'clock in the morning'.
In the 1871 census 58 year old Ann (b. 1813 in Cornwall) is recorded as living at Centenary Row, with her 30 year old daughter and two grandchildren. Bodmin Bridewell records show that earlier again, in 1855, Ann was sentenced to 6 weeks hard labour for professing to tell fortunes. At the time it was her first offence. The record describes her as *Age 42, ht 5-4?, hazel eyes, brown hair, sallow complexion, cannot read/write, single, 1 base chd. Scar on forehead & right cheek, upper front teeth project, face falls in, long visage.*

Fortune telling at Redruth (1876)

FORTUNE - TELLING AT REDRUTH.

Redruth is making progress in the wrong direction. Notwithstanding the exceeding dullness of trade, a large number of low public-houses and beershops continue to flourish ; and, despite the vigilance of the police and the abundant labours of the town-missionary, there are still in our midst numerous houses of ill-fame ; whilst no topography or directory of Redruth would be complete that omitted to mention the *habitat* of fortune-tellers, *for they literally swarm here.*

Two of this class may be consulted at almost any hour in certain courts in the principal street, and there are oracles at East End, Buller's-row, and elsewhere in the neighbourhood. Such is the effect of competition in this particular profession, that poor persons can have their planets ruled for the ridiculously low charge of twopence. There are very few servant girls at Redruth who have not

Cornish Telegraph 26.9.1876

FORTUNE - TELLING AT REDRUTH.

Redruth is making progress in the wrong direction. Notwithstanding the exceeding dullness of trade, a large number of low public-houses and beershops continue to flourish; and, despite the vigilance of the police and the abundant labours of the town-missionary, there are still in our midst numerous houses of ill-fame; whilst no topography or directory of Redruth would be complete that omitted to mention the *habitat* of fortune-tellers, *for they literally swarm here.*

Two of this class may be consulted at almost any hour in certain courts in the principal street, and there are oracles at East End, Buller's-row, and elsewhere in the neighbourhood. Such is the effect of competition in this particular profession, that poor persons can have their planets ruled for the ridiculously low charge of twopence. There are very few servant girls at Redruth who have not crossed the hands of pretended local divinators with copper or silver.

Only this week I heard of two girls having visited a fortune-teller in Fore-street. The charge (2d.) was small, but the information they received was important. In six months one of them would be married to a returned

115

emigrant having plenty of gold. The other within a few months would be the spouse of a man whose wife is now seriously ill and would soon die; and five children would be the fruit of the union. The initials of the names of both husbands in prospective were given.

This incident reminds me of a conversation on fortune-telling I happened to hear some time ago, not far from Camborne, between an old woman and an acquaintance. "We used," she said, "to visit fortune-tellers occasionally to have fun. On one occasion I was told by a witch that I should meet my future husband a few minutes after leaving the house. At the time, believing he was not at Redruth, but miles from where I was then staying, I told the old hag that she had spoken falsely; but she persisted in her assertion, and sure enough, she proved to be correct, for two minutes after leaving the house he confronted me in the street...

...But sowing hemp-seed, as it was termed,-that was the most exciting thing that ever I did. Meeting at the house of another young woman one night late, we laid the table-cloth, placed the knives and forks, bread and cheese, glasses and water, in order, and then taking some hemp-seed gradually strewed it on the hearthstone near the fire, saying the while:

"Hemp-seed I sow, hemp-seed I grow,
Let my true love come for me to mow."[70]

It was supposed that by doing this the men we were going to have (unless we were to be old maids) would come, as it were, with a scythe to mow us; at least, they would enter the room. But it was necessary to leave the front and back door open, and sit down quietly waiting until the clock struck twelve. We continued sitting until within a few minutes of that time, but just then the wind roared so awfully, and the rain poured down in such torrents that, thinking the devil was coming for us, I screamed and rushed out of the house, reaching my home half dead with fright. Of course that broke the spell."

This account was, later, rather nicely supplemented by Hammond (1895) who describes six service magicians active in Redruth including three charmers, a fortune teller who wouldn't work on Sundays, and a cunning woman, Mrs. G, who had 'clients in every grade of

---

[70] A version of the hemp seed incantation is recorded in Hunt (1865) as part of the story of Nancy Trenoweth of Penwith, who attempts to summon her lover Frank Lenine, only for him to die at sea.

society'... 'Her usual fee was three and a tanner, but small quantities of tea, flour and bacon have been accepted from the impecunious. In the seventies, and in the gloaming, her house would often be besieged by visitors. The charms she supplied them with were usually dried herbs or salt, stored in small cotton bags; these phylacteries, if worn on the chest night and day, preserved the happy possessor from bewitchment, the evil eye, bad legs, sore throats, and all manner of disease'.

An Assault: Ill-wished, Camborne (1878)

AN ASSAULT: ILL-WISHED. — Thomas Dunn was charged with assaulting Grace Williamson at Camborne. Williamson who is an old woman, appeared in Court with a black-eye and several bruises in her face, and also had marks on her arm, where the defendant had bitten her. — It appears, from the evidence, that Dunn was under the impression that he was ill-wished, and consequently, sought the aid of a woman who professed to know who did it. This said woman told him that Williamson was the woman who had ill-wished him ; and, in order to get rid of it, he must not rest until he saw her (Williamson's) blood ; and the brutal assault, for which he was summoned, was the result of this advice.—The Bench characterised the assault as a most cowardly one, and fined Dunn 7s and 18s costs.—The money was paid.

Cornish Telegraph 8.9.1878

AN ASSAULT: ILL-WISHED. – Thomas Dunn was charged with assaulting Grace Williamson at Camborne. Williamson who is an old woman, appeared in Court with a black-eye and several bruises in her face, and also had marks on her arm where the defendant had bitten her.

– It appears, from the evidence, that Dunn was under the impression that he was ill-wished, and consequently, sought the aid of a woman who professed to know who did it. This said woman told him that Williamson was the woman who had ill-wished him; and, in order to get rid of it, he must not rest until he saw her (Williamson's) blood; and the brutal assault, for which he was summoned, was the result of this advice. – The Bench characterised the assault as a most cowardly one, and fined Dunn 7s. and 18s. costs.

117

Ill-wished pig, fowls and eggs, Menheniot (1878)

SUPERSTITION —At the Liskeard County Petty Sessions, on Wednesday, Thomasine Lyne, of Menheniot, charged Jane Bennett with unlawfully beating her on the 10th of September. This was a neighbours' quarrel, and defendant was accused of ill-wishing the complainant's pig, fowls, and ducks' eggs. The defence was that Lyne, although quite a girl, had threatened to "scat Bennett's brains out" with a brick, which was produced in court, and that in self-defence Bennett struck the complainant.—The magistrates said she ought not to take the law into her own hands, and fined her 6d. and costs.

Miss K. Kaupp, R.A.M., of Liskeard, has kindly for—

RCG 27.9.1878

SUPERSTITION – At the Liskeard County Petty Sessions on Wednesday, Thomasine Lyne of Menheniot charged Jane Bennett with unlawfully beating her on the 10th September. This was a neighbours' quarrel, and defendant was accused of ill-wishing the complainants pig, fowls, and ducks' eggs.

The defence was that Lyne, although quite a girl, had threatened to 'scat Bennett's brains out' with a brick, which was produced in court, and that in self-defence Bennett struck the complainant. – The magistrates said she ought not to take the law into her own hands, and fined her 6d. and costs.

Witch bottles in Tintagel (1879)

The witch bottle as a form of magical protection became popular in the 17th century, and was endorsed e.g. by Blagrave in his 'Astrological Practice of Physick' published in 1671. The use of such bottles is now well attested throughout the UK and the US, largely due to their material nature, which has ensured they have survived up to the present day (Merrifield, 1987)[71].

FOLK LORE.
TO AVERT AN ILL WISH.

When on a walking tour through North Cornwall, I stopped to sketch a way-side cross, near Tintagel, and was informed by the farmer that it was formerly over-thrown, and on setting it up again he found several bottles full of water, with many pins in it around. On enquiring the reason of these bottles being buried, I was informed at Boscastle that "If you are ill wished, you must take a bottle, fill it with water and put some pins in it,

RCG 5.12.1879

FOLK LORE.
TO AVERT AN ILL WISH.

When on a walking tour through North Cornwall, I stopped to sketch a way-side cross, near Tintagel, and was informed by the farmer that it was formerly over- thrown, and on setting it up again he found several bottles fall of water[72], with many pins in it around. On enquiring the reason of these bottles being buried, I was informed at Boscastle that "If you are ill wished, you must take a bottle, fill it with water and put some pins in it,

---

[71] Merrifield, R. (1987). Merrifield's book refers to two bottles found several years apart in the Padstow area. The Museum of Witchcraft and Magic also has many examples of witch bottles, including a bellarmine jar from Plymouth, a club-shaped bottle from Tresillian, and two green glass bottles from Bodmin and Poughill.
[72] Likely to be a euphemism for urine.

cork it tight, and then bury it at the foot of a holy cross, and the ill wish will fall on the person who ill wished you."[73]

Witch bottles were usually hidden in and around the house, so their placement here at the foot of a wayside cross is interesting. A couple of years later, as the Cornish Telegraph explains, the vicar of St Hilary relayed a similar story to a party of visitors from Penzance:

Cornish Telegraph 13.10.1881

....the party drove through Townsend and Relubbas-where the Vicar, the Rev. S. Kingsford, received them...In the churchyard, the Vicar pointed out a cross brought in from Trevabyn, close by, where it had been used as a stepping stone for a stile. The field was known as the Cross Field.

Mr. Whitley mentioned that it was a custom for people to bury bottles of water with pins in it at the foot of such a cross to remove ill-wishes. Such bottles had been dug up.

---

[73] As Langstone (2017) explains, the author of this anecdote is H. Mitchell Whitley, and this particular cross is likely to be in Fenterleigh.

120

Mr Sirloin, Wendron (1880)

to be kept under proper control.

(From our own Correspondent).

Gross Superstition.- Mr Sirloin, a stock breeder, not a hundred miles from the Gweek River and Wendron Parish Church, having lost calves and other juvenile animals had recourse to the "wise woman" who is wise enough for his pockets to dispense charms &c., to catch fools' shillings, and in this case landed a fine fish, as Sirloin is a rich man. Nineteenth century, with all your scoff at undoubted revelation, what do you yet believe in charms and spells !

The Burials Bill is likely to go ; if so, I want to know

RCG 18.6.1880

Gross superstition. – Mr Sirloin a stock breeder not a hundred miles from the Gweek River and Wendron Parish Church having lost calves and other juvenile animals had recourse the "wise woman" who is wise enough for his pockets to dispense charms &c., to catch fools' shillings, and in this case landed a fine fish, as Sirloin is a rich man. Nineteenth century with all your scoff at undoubted revelation, what do you yet believe in charms and spells!

Death of a Cornish Witch (1880)

DEATH OF A REPUTED CORNISH WITCH.

An extraordinary but well-authenticated instance of belief in witchcraft comes from St. Blazey, Cornwall. A woman named Keam, who died the other day, was believed by her neighbours to be a witch, and great difficulty was experienced in getting any-one to bear her to her last resting-

121

place. It was feared, in fact, that the funeral would have had to have been postponed; but, at the last moment, several bricklayers, who happened to be at work in the neighbourhood, were induced to lay down their tools, and carry the coffin to church in their shirt-sleeves. After the service a like difficulty was experienced in getting the coffin to the grave, and that duty had, at length, to be done in a very irregular way.

The decease of the witch, it is said, had apparently lifted a weight from the minds of many weak persons, one cripple asserting that he shall now recover, and should ever have been a cripple had she not ill-wished him[74].

Mary Ivey's Picture Machine (1880)

THREE MONTHS IN GAOL FOR A CURER OF ILL-WISHING.

SINGULAR CUNNING AND SUPERSTITION

At our town-hall, on Tuesday, before Messrs. G. Michell and G. J. Smith, Mary Ann Ivey was charged with unlawfully obtaining from Grace Tippett, of Pool, £40, with intent to defraud her.

Mr. J. R. DANIELL defended.

Prosecutrix, a widow, said :—On Easter Monday I was chastising my daughter, when defendant came into the house and said I was doing wrong, and ought to desist, she having a secret to tell me. On the following evening she came again, and we both went upstairs. She said there was an ill-wish gone over the girl, and it was a fearful one ; likewise every one of my children. She then said, " Your husband was killed, and you will have more than him. Your are grieving about the boy Jimmy, but he will never go to the Militia unless the wish is stopped." I then asked defendant how she knew of such matters. Prisoner replied that when left a widow she and her children went into the Truro Union, and whilst there she attended a gipsy woman, who told her how to perform cures against ill-wishing, and she (prisoner) had a machine which had a face like a small clock, with hands, and which, when worked would bring up small pictures, to work which would require some chemicals, which were procured at Redruth, and placed in the machine with a funnel. Also she had a case in hand, and which was nearly finished, the result of which so pleased the parties that they gave her son £15 to take him to America, and she

Cornishman 27.5.1880

---

[74] Parish burial records indicate this was Catharine Keam, 'a reputed witch' who was 59 when she died (i.e. born in 1821).

THREE MONTHS IN GAOL FOR A CURER OF ILL-WISHING. SINGULAR CUNNING AND SUPERSTITION

At our town-hall (Camborne), on Tuesday...Mary Ann Ivey was charged with unlawfully obtaining from Grace Tippett of Pool, £40, with intent to defraud her.

Prosecutrix, a widow, said: - On Easter Monday I was chastising my daughter, when defendant (Mary Ivey) came into the house and said I was doing wrong, and ought to desist, she having a secret to tell me.

On the following evening she came again, and we both went upstairs. She said there was an ill-wish gone over the girl, and it was a fearful one; likewise every one of my children. She then said, "Your husband was killed, and you will have more than him. You are grieving about the boy Jimmy but he will never go to the Militia unless the wish is stopped".

I then asked defendant how she knew of such matters. Prisoner replied that when left a widow she and her children went into the Truro Union, and whilst there she attended a gipsy woman, who told her how to perform cures against ill-wishing, and she (prisoner) had a machine which had a face like a small clock, with hands, and which, when worked would bring up small pictures, to work which would require some chemicals, which were procured at Redruth, and placed in the machine with a funnel.

Also she had a case in hand, and which was nearly finished, the result of which so pleased the parties that they gave her son £15 to take him to America, and she thought that my family could be cured for £5. I pawned my daughter's watch for £1, and gave it to the prisoner as a first instalment. The following day I went to Truro and drew £5 from the bank, which was given to her, £1 at a time daily.

She then told me it would take £7 more, which money I paid her. £4 was paid at one time. She then told me the case was so heavy that she could not make it start for that money. I then drew £10 more and gave to prisoner in £2 instalments. It went on until I had drawn £35 from the bank, the whole of which money was paid within six weeks. The last money paid was on the 10th of May, when she told me that was the finishing of the witchcraft.

In the meanwhile she told me if I didn't carry out what she directed it would not surprise her if my daughter was to find me dead in the street.

She had small pieces of the garments of the children and also some portion of their hair, which was taken from them whilst they were asleep, and said that every night she took the case before the Lord, as she found it quite right to release the fatherless children from the bondage laid on them...

....The bench were of the opinion that the charge was fully proved against the prisoner and she should be committed to gaol for 3 months heavy labour.

Ill-wishing as retribution, Gwennap (1881)

EAST KERRIER PETTY SESSIONS.—These sessions were held in the Town-hall, on Wednesday last, before Mr. M. H. Williams (chairman), Capt. Norway, R.N., and Messrs. Beauchamp and Kelly. A gipsy woman, named Small, was charged with telling fortunes in the parish of Gwennap. J. Dowerick stated that he paid her at different times 12s. 6d., and when he would not give her any more money she "ill-wished" him, and he believed that accounted for the illness he had suffered since February last. The Bench inflicted a fine of £5 and 7s. cost, or two months' imprisonment. The money was paid.—John Coplin, of Falmouth, was

Cornish Echo (Falmouth Times) 30.4.1881

EAST KERRIER PETTY SESSIONS.- These sessions were held in the Town-hall, on Wednesday last...A gipsy woman, named Small[75], was charged with telling fortunes in the parish of Gwennap.

J. Dowerick stated that he paid her at different times 12s. 6d., and when he would not give her any more money she "ill-wished" him, and he believed that accounted for the illness he had suffered since February last. The Bench inflicted a fine of £5 and 7s. cost, or two months' imprisonment. The money was paid.

---

[75] See entry 'Gipsies in Trouble' (1867) concerning Gentilla Small. It is not clear whether this is the same person.

Professor of Palmistry, St Austell (1881)

direct from the Board-room.

POLICE COURT. WEDNESDAY.—Before Mr Arthur Code, an old woman named Bessie Foster, aged 70, was charged with endeavouring to extort money from a domestic servant in the employ of Mr Parsons, of Lower Trewbiddle, St Austell, by pretending to tell the girl's fortune. For informing this very credulous servant that "she would be married to a Frenchman with lots of money," the old woman, a short time since, received 1s 6d. However, on the present occasion, Police-Sergeant Thomas heard from an adjoining room the promise of further good news for 2s 6d, and at once took charge of the aged "professor of palmistry." She was sent to prison for fourteen days. Paul Nicholls, an old offender, who has just been released from prison, was charged

RCG 18.2.1881

POLICE COURT. WEDNESDAY. - Before Mr Arthur Code, an old woman named Bessie Foster, aged 70, was charged with endeavouring to extort money from a domestic servant in the employ of Mr Parsons, of Lower Trewbiddle, St Austell, by pretending to tell the girl's fortune.

For informing this very credulous servant that "she would be married to a Frenchman with lots of money," the old woman, a short time since, received 1s. 6d. However, on the present occasion, Police-Sergeant Thomas heard from an adjoining room the promise of further good news for 2s. 6d., and at once took charge of the aged "professor of palmistry." She was sent to prison for fourteen days.

Ann 'Granny' Boswell, Camborne 1882

There are well over twenty articles in the Cornish newspapers relating to Ann or 'Granny' Boswell (1813 – 1909) and her family[76], especially clustered around the year 1883 when, following a violent assault on the road near Cubert, her 18 year old son Abraham was convicted of manslaughter and given a twenty year prison sentence. Granny Boswell's speculative biography was first compiled by Kelvin Jones in 1998 (c.f. Jones, 2015), and, as a result she is often described as a wise woman or pellar, very much in the mould of Tammy Blee[77]. In fact there are no newspaper articles that support this view, and with the exception of the following short piece, none that mention her working as a service magician. Instead she is usually described as a 'licensed hawker', whose multiple court appearances and prison sentences were almost all for drunkenness and begging (see Appendix E for examples). Certainly, though, she was a well-known, semi-legendary figure in West Cornwall, and is referred to as the 'Mother of the Gipsies' in one of the articles[78]. Despite apparently smoking and drinking to excess, she lived to a grand old age, and was buried with her husband Ephraim in Tregerest cemetery near Newbridge, between Penzance and St Just.

EXTRAORDINARY FORTUNE TELLING. — At the Guildhall, on Tuesday, before the Mayor (R. R. Victor) and F. Boase, Esqs., Ann Boswell, aged 61, a licensed hawker, of Camborne, was charged with having begged alms in Penzance on the previous day. Defendant pleaded guilty. It appeared from a statement of Superintendent Olds that the defendant was in the habit of introducing herself into people's houses on pretence of telling their fortunes. She then saw something which she fancied, and said, You will give me this, won't you? and the circumstances had such an effect on persons that they allowed the

Cornish Telegraph 2.12.1882

---

[76] The earliest article relating to Ann Boswell is from 1863. Ann, under the influence of drink, was accused of assaulting her husband in Penzance.

[77] The four or five charms Ann is reputed to have used were actually taken from the first two volumes of Old Cornwall magazine. In truth, given her Irish Romany background, it seems unlikely she would have used such traditional Cornish remedies.

[78] But not as *Queen of the Gipsies* as has been claimed. According to news reports from 1883, Ann's husband Ephraim was father to 16 children, and his father was known as Old Boswell 'King of the Gipsies'. Cornish parish records indicate that Ann herself was 5ft1, born in Tipperary, 'had no education', and whilst living in Cornwall gave birth to five children, the first being born in 1861.

EXTRAORDINARY FORTUNE TELLING....Ann Boswell, aged 61, a licensed hawker, of Camborne, was charged with having begged alms in Penzance on the previous day. Defendant pleaded guilty.

It appeared from a statement of Superintendent Olds that the defendant was in the habit of introducing herself into people's houses on pretence of telling their fortunes. She then saw something which she fancied, and said, "You will give me this, won't you?" and the circumstances had such an effect on persons that they allowed the defendant to take the articles away. Two jugs, a cup and saucer and plate, and a marmalade jar, which the prisoner had obtained in this manner, were laid before the Court.

P.C. 4 (Thomas) stated that Mrs Penhalligon, of South Terrace, had told him that the defendant entered the house and wanted to tell her fortune. Defendant asked for money, but Mrs Penhalligon refused to give her any. Defendant then went to a cupboard, and seeing there the glass jug produced, she said, "Will you be so kind as to give me this?" Mrs Penhalligon, feeling very nervous[79], did not say yes or no, and defendant then put the jug in her apron and took it away, leaving a comb with one of Mrs Penhalligon's children.

Mrs Penhalligon, however, refused to keep the comb, and returned it by witness, who had called at several other places and found that the defendant wanted a cup and saucer, a jug, a penny for good luck, or anything she could get.-

The Mayor said that the defendant was liable to three months' imprisonment, but in consideration of her age, she would only be committed for a fortnight.-

---

[79] The Cornishman article covering the same story is, tellingly, entitled 'Fear of a Gipsy's Ill-wishes'. According to a document held by the Museum of Cornish Life in Helston, Boswell, in 1906, is reported to have ill-wished a car that had honked its horn at her. Shortly afterwards one of its steel tension rods broke (Jones, 2015).

Phrenology (1883)

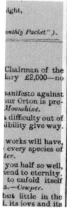

PHRENOLOGY.

SIR,—I think phrenology is either in its infancy or devoid of a scientific basis.

Some years since I was curious enough to spend a trifle of money with a phrenologist, who professed to define my capabilities by examining the organs of my head. On investigating the organs of my head, he gave me what he termed a "chart." In less than twelve months after this "farce" I called again, and had another chart. This latter "chart" was so totally different from the "former," that I was at once led to conclude that "phrenology was grounded on an assumed hypothesis, no less phantastical and absurd than "astrology," which is a mere myth of antiquity.

In my youthful days I had read the works of Dr. Gall and Combe, the former who was the founder of this so-called science, and the latter the president of the Phrenological Society ; and, really, Sir, to be candid on the matter, notwithstanding all the fine technical terms used by these worthies in arguing the infallibility of their observations, I could but regard their deductions as the wild dreams of men who had blindly fallen into a ludicrous absurdity. That I may not be thought vain and pedantic on this point, let me be understood to say, that I do not attribute to these men—men who have engraved their names in the tablets of history—a want of knowledge as anatomists, but most certainly to those who have

RCG 20.4.1883

PHRENOLOGY.

SIR, I think phrenology is either in its infancy or devoid of a scientific basis.

Some years since I was curious enough to spend a trifle of money with a phrenologist, who professed to define my capabilities by examining the organs of my head. On investigating the organs of my head, he gave me what he termed a "chart." In less than twelve months after this "farce" I called again, and had another chart. This latter" chart" was so totally different from the "former," that I was at once led to conclude that "phrenology was grounded on an assumed hypothesis, no less phantastical and absurd than "astrology," which is a mere myth of antiquity.

...phrenology, if not grounded on a like basis with necromancy, is equally ridiculous and absurd.

Yours faithfully, Dated Truro, April 16th, 1883.
REFORMER.

A 'Challenge' in Redruth (1883)

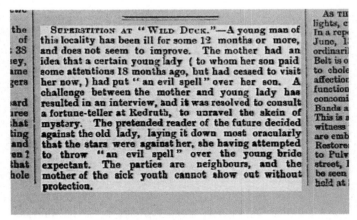

The Cornishman 24.5.1883

SUPERSTITION AT "WILD DUCK." - A young man of this locality has been ill for some 12 months or more, and does not seem to improve. The mother had an idea that a certain young lady (to whom her son paid some attentions 18 months ago, but had ceased to visit her now,) had put "an evil spell" over her son. A challenge between the mother and young lady has resulted in an interview, and it was resolved to consult a fortune-teller at Redruth, to unravel the skein of mystery.

The pretended reader of the future decided against the old lady (mother), laying it down most oracularly that the stars were against her, she having attempted to throw "an evil spell" over the young bride expectant. The parties are neighbours, and the mother of the sick youth cannot show out without protection.

Horse sacrifice (1883)[80]

SUPERSTITIONS DIE HARD.—A horse died the other day on a farm in the neighbourhood of St. Ives. Its carcase was dragged, on a Sunday, away up to the granite rock-basins and weather worn bosses of Trecroben and there burnt—in order to drive away the evil spell, or ill-wishing, which afflicted the farm to which the animal belonged!

The Cornishman 1.2.1883

SUPERSTITIONS DIE HARD. - A horse died the other day on a farm in the neighbourhood of St. Ives.

Its carcase was dragged, on a Sunday, away up to the granite rock-basins and weather worn bosses of Trecroben (Trencrom) and there burnt-in order to drive away the evil spell, or ill-wishing, which afflicted the farm to which the animal belonged!

Paying for an ill-wish, Camborne (1884)

Cunning folk, typically, offered to reverse the effects of ill-wishing. However some, for the right price, could also be persuaded to work malefic magic.

ILL-WISHING.—The belief in witchcraft has not entirely died out. A certain woman who lives in Camborne, and who professes to be a true Christian, not liking the idea of her son (who is abroad) sending home money to his wife, lately went to a so-called witch and gave her a fee of 1s 6d, so that her daughter-in-law might be ill-wished.

THE DWELLINGS OF THE POOR.—The Royal Co-

Cornish Telegraph 1.5.1884

---

[80] This short report was later republished in Courtney's *Cornish Feasts and Folklore* (1890).

ILL-WISHING.-The belief in witchcraft has not entirely died out. A certain woman who lives in Camborne, and who professes to be a true Christian, not liking the idea of her son (who is abroad) sending home money to his wife, lately went to a so-called witch and gave her a fee of 7s. 6d. so that her daughter-in-law might be ill-wished.

Illogan Assault (1887)

voluntary wreckers.

CORNWALL is one of the few counties where a belief in witchcraft still survives in spite of the School Board. The East Penwith magistrates had last week to consider a charge of assault preferred by an Illogan woman against a neighbour, who had accused her of "ill-wishing her children." But we are informed on excellent authority that Illogan is not the only place in the county which boasts of a real or suspected "dealer in magic and spells." Some of these witches are "white" and some "black," but both orders are

Cornish Telegraph 9.6.1887

CORNWALL is one of the few counties where a belief in witchcraft still survives in spite of the School Board. The East Penwith magistrates had last week to consider a charge of assault preferred by an Illogan woman against a neighbour, who had accused her of "ill-wishing her children."

But we are informed on excellent authority that Illogan is not the only place in the county which boasts of a real or suspected "dealer in magic and spells." Some of these witches are "white" and some "black," but both orders are made to lend themselves to the commission of "deeds without a name."

Seeing blood, Camborne (1887)[81]

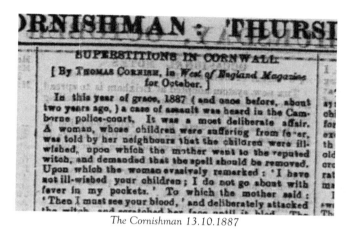

The Cornishman 13.10.1887

SUPERSTITIONS IN CORNWALL
[By THOMAS CORNISH, in West of England Magazine]

In this year of grace, 1887 (and once before, about two years ago,) a case of assault was heard in the Camborne police-court. It was a most deliberate affair. A woman, whose children were suffering from fever, was told by her neighbours that the children were ill- wished, upon which the mother went to the reputed witch, and demanded that the spell should be removed. Upon which the woman evasively remarked: 'I have not ill-wished your children; I do not go about with fever in my pockets'. To which the mother said: 'Then I must see your blood,' and deliberately attacked the witch, and scratched her face until it bled.

The superstition is that if a witch refuses to take off a spell, the persons demanding it must see the blood of the witch. In the first case the witch was a man. I find that a similar superstition occurs in North Britain, but there it is the person bewitched who must see the blood of the witch.

---

[81] This story is mentioned by Hamilton Jenkin (1933), who also outlines a similar incident in Morvah, as well as a more recent story of ill-wishing from 1929.

Story of an ill-wished family (1887)

The Cornishman 17.3.1887

The following story is fresh from the mint. I had it related to-day by one of the family on which the ill-wish was said to have fallen. It was given in perfectly good faith and simplicity, and I will relate it, very nearly, in her own words. I make no comment, but it seems very strange.

Well, it was in this way. My father lived upon a little farm, and old Robin, as he was called, had a little farm joining to ours, and near our house there was a field, with only a hedge between that and a field belonging to Old Robin, and he hardly ever kept his gaps stopped, so that the pigs from one field were often found running into the other, and, of course, our pigs would sometimes stray into Old Robin's field, and he was a cross old fellow and would fuss and throw stones to the pigs.

So, one day, our great sow walked into old Robin's field without asking by your leave, and out comes Old Robin, swearing like a man-of-war, and began to throw stones at the sow: and when mother saw that she ran out and told Old Robin to stop and he wouldn't, but kept on throwing stones to the sow, and then mother took up a stone and said, "If you don't stop throwing stones to that sow I'll throw one to your head and scat your skull

134

in"; and then he stopped, and he went off grumbling and saying, "Never mind, I'll make you smart for that; you'll wish your cake dough, you will."

We didn't think very much about it, but one day, when we was boiling a great pan and water for washing the clothes, two little children that was playing near the pan of water pulled it over upon them and, after suffering a great deal, they both died.

Well, of course that might all be, and might happen to we so well as to anybody else; but, a short time after that, three young calves sickened and died one after the other, and then a heifer was took sick and we began to think that everything wasn't right and we was feeling very strange and queer about it; and some of the neighbours begun to say that it looked suspicious and they should like to know whether Old Robin didn't know more about it than be would tell. The children and the cattle are surely ill-wished, and so on.

Soon after that a great pig was took sick and left his meat and died without so much as the butcher's eyes being set upon it, much less anything else he could do to it, and so they persuaded father to go to Helston to see the Pellar.

You know at that time the Pellar was a woman, but she is dead a good bit ago[82]. So father went to the Pellar, and when she opened the dear to him she called him by his right name and told him what he was come for and all about the children that was scalded and the cattle that died-the calves and the heifer and the pig; and I'm sure she couldn't have known him and nobody could have told her about the children and the cattle; but she said You have got a heavy wish laid upon you a very heavy wish indeed; and you have suffered a good deal.

Then he said 'Can you help me?' She said 'Yes I can; your enemy is of your place and your own relations' (for Old Robin was a relation to my father.) So she said she must take the ill-wish from him and his family and his cattle, and lay it on them belonging to Old Robin.

---

[82] Almost certainly a reference to Tammy Blee who died in 1856.

135

And then she brought out six little black silk bags, and told him to tie one of them round his neck by a piece of black ribbon and keep the other bags, for fear he might lose the one from his neck. So he hanged the bag about his neck and we had nothing particular amiss after that, but the wish fell upon Old Robin's hosses, for he had a good many hosses, Old Robin had, and the hosses' feet begun to swell and they swelled to that degree that they was so big as over-grown turmats[83]; and, you believe me, we used to feel quite sorry to hear the poor hosses dragging their great feet over the rough stones. Twas quite pitiful to see and to hear them.

Astrology or Planet Ruling – Two ads (1888)

Cornish & Devon Post 7.1.1888

Cornish & Devon Post 10.3.1888

1888 saw J W Hershell of Somerset place numerous ads in the Cornish and Devon Post. G. Singer, also from Somerset, used an almost identical format.

---

[83] Turnips?

Fortune by post (1888)

The author of 'The Astrologer of the Nineteenth Century' (1826), Robert Cross Smith, died in 1832. During the last years of his life he also produced the almanack 'The Prophetic Messenger'. Both titles, for which he adopted the name 'Raphael', were important to the Victorian revival of astrology. The following advert is likely to have been placed by an astrologer local to Launceston who was assuming his identity.

READ THIS.

YOUR FORTUNE set forth by **RAPHAEL**, " the great **ASTROLOGER** of the Nineteenth Century," who now sojourns for a time in the West of England, affording you a description of your partner for life, with a needful advice, that you can require, by sending to your " Newspaper Office, Launceston," on closed letter to Raphael, containing your time of birth, —or as near to it as you possibly can, and a postal order for half-a-crown ; when a parcel of all letters will be sent to Raphael once a week, and in another week you will receive by regular postal delivery, your reply—at your residence. Please enclose a stamp for prompt reply.

WONDERFULLY CHEAP PRINTING for Cash.

Cornish & Devon Post 14.1.1888

Fortune Teller, Stokeclimsland (1889)

THE FORTUNE TELLER AT STOKECLIMSLAND.

Bessie James, a travelling gipsy, was at Callington, on Monday, charged with stealing in March, April, and May last, a silver bracelet, locket, silver watch and gold chain, silk dress and bangle, the property of Emily Clarendon Keast, of Stokeslimsland.

Prisoner, a hawker of brushes, called at the house where prosecutrix lodged in March and told her she was ill-wished and was ill, and if she would give her money she could do her good by working the planets. As she had no money prisoner asked for her trinkets and jewellery as they would do as well. Prosecutrix said foolishly she could have a necklet, locket, and bracelet on condition that they were returned sometime in April.

Prisoner called again and said the articles were not valuable enough to turn of the planet book, and prosecutrix let her have her gold chain which was also to be returned with the other things.

In May prisoner came with her mother from Jersey, Prisoner said her mother was very clever and considered prosecutrix very lucky girl in securing her services. Then prisoner had her gold ring and a black lace dress and said she would come back in about a mouth and return the goods, when she was to be paid for telling her fortune. Although prosecutrix said she waited patiently prisoner did not return. She was apprehended by Inspector Philp at Launceston on Tuesday.

Prisoner first denied and afterwards admitted receiving the goods, but said she had not got them now. On Thursday two persons came to prosecutrix's house and handed back some of the goods and 5s. in lieu of the bracelet, which was lost.-Mrs. Freedman, of Penzance, daughter of a pawnbroker, produced a bangle which was pawned by prisoner and identified by prosecutrix.

The prisoner pleaded guilty and was sentenced to one month's hard labour.

Mrs Clarke and the Jelbert brothers, Penzance (1890)

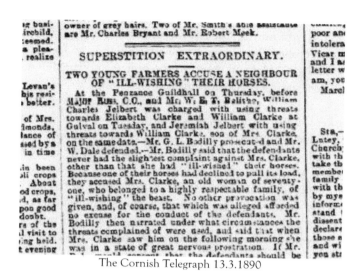

The Cornish Telegraph 13.3.1890

Living in Gulval just outside Penzance, Mrs Clarke, a farmers wife, was accused of ill-wishing her neighbour's horses. This story is another that circulated widely outside Cornwall, and is remarkable for the detailed evidence recorded in the newspaper, only a fraction of which is reproduced here:

EXTRAORDINARY BELIEF IN WITCH-CRAFT AND ILL-WISHING

Mrs. Clarke stated that she was the wife of Mr. Joseph Clarke, farmer, and was seventy-one years of age. She had never had any quarrels with the Jelberts, though the defendants had several times accused her of ill-wishing their horses.

Mr. Bodilly: To clear that up once for all, do you know how to do it (i.e. ill-wish)?

Complainant: No.

Mr. Bodilly: You are not a witch by profession?

Complainant: I should not like to be.

Continuing, complainant said that on Tuesday night she was sitting at the table with her husband, when they heard a loud knocking at the door. She opened it, and found the two defendants there. William Charles Jelbert said, "Come out, you devil, I will wait no longer, I will murder you." She said: "Before you murder me tell me what it is for." And defendant replied "You have ill-wished our horses to kick, and I will murder you to-night." Her son went for the police, and the defendants went away, after beating their sticks against the door.

Joseph Clarke, Gulval, farmer, husband of the complainant, said that about seven o'clock on Tuesday night he was getting his supper, when he heard a loud knock at the door His wife went to the door, and when it was opened witness saw the two Jelberts, William Charles had a big stick in his hand. He threatened to cut witness' wife in two, and also to "send her to hell." Jelbert had once told witness when on the road to Penzance, that his horse would not pull, and added. "You do know how." Witness said that he did not understand what defendant meant, and asked him for an explanation but all that he could get out of him was "You do know how."-

Mr. Bodilly: How old are you?
Jelbert: Twenty-five.
Have you been to school?
Yes.
And you, an educated Englishman of twenty-five, pledge your oath that you believe in ill-wishing!?
Yes sir, I do.
How is it done!?
I do not know what way it is done, but it is done -
And do I understand that every time you have a jibbing horse, you say it is ill-wished?
Yes, sir. I know it -
In what other way does it show that it is ill-wished?
Sometimes it will go as well as usual, and at others we cannot get it on.- Major
Ross: Are you sure as to who is the ill-wisher?
Jelbert: I do think, sir,
Mr. Bodilly: On this day your mare kicked?
Yes -

And with that quickness of perception for when you are remarkable, you said that Mrs. Clarke had ill-wished it?

Yes -

How do you connect the kicking of your mare with Ms. Clarke?

She is always peeping at the horse, and watching it-

Then you are a believer in the evil eye?

Yes, sir....

The Jelberts, seen as 'harbouring a delusion' and believing in 'utter rubbish', were let off with a warning by the court. The same edition of the paper carried the following comments on the case, however:

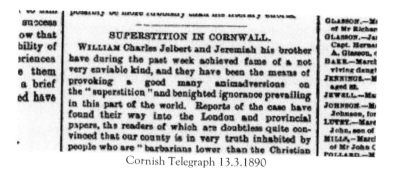

SUPERSTITION IN CORNWALL.

WILLIAM Charles Jelbert and Jeremiah his brother have during the past week achieved fame of a not very enviable kind, and they have been the means of provoking a good many animadversions on the " superstition "and benighted ignorance prevailing in this part of the world. Reports of the case have found their way into the London and provincial papers, the readers of which are doubtless quite convinced that our county is in very truth inhabited by people who are " barbarians lower than the Christian

Cornish Telegraph 13.3.1890

...We have been informed on very good authority of an even more remarkable case than that of the brothers Jelbert, which occurred not long ago in a neighbouring village. A farmer imagined that he had been "ill wished," and after battling for some time against the mysterious hostile influence, he gave up the contest in despair, and actually left his holding!

This is not the only case that has recently come under our notice. We heard the other day of another farmer, who was firmly convinced that his cattle had come under the ban of some enchantress, but as he had not been able to discover the culprit, he was anxious to keep the fact secret. Whether he has by this time succeeded in tracing out the "witch" we cannot say. If he has, he will do well to think twice before imitating the example set by the Jelberts.

Cattle seem to be the favourite victims of the Cornish witches, but they do not confine their attentions to four-footed creatures. A case was heard at the East Penwith Petty Sessions some two years ago in which a woman who was summoned for assaulting her neighbour, pleaded in defence that the complainant had "ill- wished" her children: the assault had a definite object-to draw the blood of the "witch." This is supposed to immediately break the spell, and to restore the victims to their normal condition. It is inevitable that where any considerable section of the population labour under such delusions, there should be a certain number of sharp rogues ready to profit by the folly of their fellows.

This is the case in several places in West Cornwall, where "witches" still practise the "black art," and are believed to make a very comfortable livelihood out of the credulity and weakness of their neighbours. How are these obstinate remnants of ancient poisonous growths to be finally eradicated from the minds of our Cornish, peasantry? Education apparently cannot do it, for many of the latter day believers in witchcraft have passed their standards; religion cannot do it, for the Cornish people are more religious than the inhabitants of many localities where superstitions of this particular kind are practically unknown. Nay, their religious convictions, their belief in the letter of the Bible, will sometimes serve to confirm them in their faith in what may be called the vulgarised supernatural. "There was a witch of Endor" they will say, "and why not a witch of Gulval, Helston, or St. Just?"

It seems to us that much might be done by the individual efforts of the clergy, the Nonconformist ministers, and the local preachers. If they would take the trouble to investigate any cases of alleged "ill-wishing" which may come to their notice, if they would endeavour to discover the real cause of the calamities which the sufferers attribute to enemies armed which superhuman powers, if they would reason with the victims and impress upon them the folly and wickedness of their insensate belief, the final extinction of these miserable superstitions might be effected in a generation. And now, having said our say about Cornish superstition, we may be permitted to remind our superior critics that there are people in

142

other parts of the country who are the victims of delusions quite as gross as a belief in the power of a harmless old woman to cause a horse to kick. Are not the well-dressed and well-educated people who sit in the dark round a table, and listen open-mouthed to the knocks which a long-haired swindler called a medium assures them are a communication from somebody's great grandmother, immeasurably more contemptible than the uncultured Cornish peasants who retain some vestiges of the old beliefs that have descended from generation to generation, and have become associated with localities with which they have been familiar throughout their lives? Spiritualism is an infinitely more stupid and vulgar form of superstition than a belief in witchcraft, which at all events has something romantic....

A Score of Cury bullocks (1890)

lodge, hived a fine swarm of bees on Sunday. May 18.

A GRATIFYING success attended the volunteer bazaar held a few days since at Truro. Over £500 was realised.

A SCORE of Cury bullocks being 'ill-wished' a Camborne charmer has removed the spell and the herd is doing well.

THE wreck of the *Brankelow*, at Gunwalloe, has again been sold, the price this time reaching over £1,000. The purchaser is a Mr King, of Manchester.

The Cornishman 29.5.1890

A SCORE of Cury bullocks being 'ill-wished' a Camborne charmer has removed the spell and the herd is doing well.

'A Fortune Teller Entrapped', St Mawes (1891)

This article describes an example of the 'entrapment' of a magical practitioner who went by the name of Raffalonious. In this case the daughter of a local policeman posed as a client for the fortune teller:

A FORTUNE-TELLER ENTRAPPED.

HEAVY PENALTY.

For some time an advertisement appeared in the *Western Chronicle*, published at Yeovil, to the effect that a man styling himself Raffalonious, the great astrologer of the East, and sojourning in the West of England, would cast anyone's horoscope on receipt of a postal order for 2s. 6d., a stamp for prompt reply, applicant having only to state time of birth as near as possible and the

Superintendent Philp, in the course of his evidence, produced the following advertisement which had appeared in the *Western Chronicle:—*

"YOUR PLANET RULED,"

By Raffalonious, the Great Astrologer of the East, who now sojourns for a time in the West of England, and by whom you may have your Horoscope cast, and all things of importance pertaining to you fully depicted, with results, and all the important affairs of life fully shown; by your enclosing a postal order for 2s. 6d and a stamp for prompt reply and by your stating your time of Birth as near as possible, and the County of your birthplace.—To "J. R. B.," Agent, St. Mawes, Cornwall. Emigration advised upon, &c., &c.

His attention having been called to the above,

Royal Cornwall Gazette 23.5.1891

For some time an advertisement appeared in the Western Chronicle, published at Yeovil, to the effect that a man styling himself 'Raffalonious, the Great Astrologer of the East', and sojourning in the West of England, would cast anyone's horoscope on receipt of a postal order for 2s. 6d., a stamp for prompt reply, applicant having only to state time of birth as near as possible and the county of birth, the advertisement directed persons to apply to "J.R.B.," agent, St. Mawes, Cornwall.

Superintendent Philp, of Truro, was brought acquainted with the above, and he at once took steps to discover the author of the advertisement[84]. With the assistance of Superintendent Williams it was ascertained that the individual in question was Russel Bosisto, residing at Windmill Cottage, St. Just Lane, St. Mawes.

---

[84] It seems odd that Superintendent Philp noticed the ad in the Somerset-based Western Chronicle, as Raffalonious placed nearly 100 ads in newspapers based in the Southwest between 1888-1891, and the majority were actually in the Cornish newspapers.

144

Superintendent Philp then arranged with Miss Lily Rosevear, of Falmouth, and his daughter to visit Bosisto, which they did on Friday, the 15th instant. The two young ladies paid their half-crown, and each received the "ruling of the planets."

A warrant was obtained by Superintendent Philp for Bosisto's arrest which was carried into effect. He was conveyed to Tregony police station and was brought before the Rev. A. R. Tomlinson and Messrs. T. H. Vyryan and J. G. Moor on Friday, charged with having unlawfully pretended to tell fortunes, and to deceive and impose on Lillie Rosevear and others, her Majesty's subject.

Superintendent Philp, in the course of his evidence, produced the following advertisement which had appeared in the Western Chronicle:-

"YOUR PLANET RULED,"
By Raffalonious, the Great Astrologer of the East, who now sojourns for a time in the West of England, and by whom you may have your Horoscope cast, and all things of importance pertaining to you fully depicted, with results, and all the important affairs of life fully shown; by your enclosing postal order for 2s. 6d and a stamp for prompt reply and by your stating your time of Birth as near as possible, and the County of your birthplace .- To "J. R. B., Agent, St. Mawes, Cornwall. Emigration advised upon[85], &c., &c.

...Lily Roseveare stated that she lived at Falmouth, and on Friday, the 15th instant, in company with Miss Bessie Philp, she went to the prisoner's house...
...Witness proceeded - He said he could not tell my fortune at once because he would have to work it out by figures, and he also asked me the year I was born, the time and date of my birth, and added that he would tell me my future partner for life (laughter). He demanded 2s. 6d. and a penny stamp, which I paid him. He said he would post the information to

---

[85] Many families from Cornwall were emigrating at the end of the 19th century, because of the collapse of the mining industry. There was much uncertainty as to what their future held.

Falmouth Post-office in a day or two, in a letter addressed to Miss B. Farrant...

...Supt. Philp said: I apprehended the prisoner at St. Just-in-Roseland, under a warrant, at his house. I read the warrant to him, and he replied "Yes, I know it, and it's done a great deal up the country." I told him it was in regard to an interview he had with two young women giving the name of Farrant. Prisoner replied, "Yes, they came here, and I sent the result to the Post-office at Falmouth." ....

I brought him to the police-station at Tregony, and there searched him, and found on him £1 10s. in gold, a half-crown, and a 2s. piece in silver. The half-crown bore the mark I put on it before handing it to my daughter. I told him it was one of the coins I had marked. I also found on the prisoner 11 postal orders, amounting to 19s., bearing the following postal towns - Finsbury, St. Giles, Dorset, Warminster, Sturminster, Kingston-on-Thames, Guildford, East Penard, Ottery St. Mary, Cambridge and Ely. I also found nine advertisements with, reference to ruling planets, having the initials J R. B., and postage stamps amounting to 58. 8d.

The magistrates fined prisoner £2 10s, and costs 15s. 6d. in each case; in all £6 11. Prisoner said he thought be bad been very leniently dealt with, but added that what he told the young ladies was as true as the Bible. He also wished to know if he could again practice anything of the sort, and the magistrates informed him that he could not, and if he again came before them they would deal much more severely with him.

The Bench expressed themselves well pleased with the manner in which the case had been got up, and said credit was due to Supt. Philp and to the young ladies.

'Bottled up' in Brea (1892)

THE CO

LL.

olidated
Foster,
Alverne-
rnoon.
re were
tho. W.
. Gryils,
illyams,
d, John
n. John
W. H.
lett, and
tary.

for the
nts, and
for bad
ises, and
nts to
ncluding
profit of

FIRM BELIEF IN ILL-WISHING.

THE BOTTLE AND PIN CHARM.

The Spell Removed And The Spellbound Better.

' When will a belief in witchcraft, the evil eye, ill-wishing, and other *diablerie* die out in Cornwall?' is the oft
repeated question among its more enlightened people. In
an old house near Brea, Camborne, this week, some bottles,
filled with filthy liquid and pins, were found in a chimney
that required repair.   The bottles were smashed ; and an
old woman, who had been confined to her house for a long
time, her residence being close to the chimney find, declared she had relief instantly the bottles were broken, for
she was sure she was ' bottled-up ' by another old woman,
who lived in the said house.
(She, by the way, is getting a rough time of it at the hands
of believers in the Black Art.)
   The poor old crone, thus suspected, vehemently protests
her freedom from any malice whatever toward her neighbours or any one else ; and avers that she had no knowledge
of any bottles being lodged in her chimney.
   The old woman who has been a sufferer for so long a
time has since, o ing to her joy at the discovery and destruction of the bottles, and at her triumph over her suspected

A

The
the Te
accorc
Cornis
mines
   Mr
suffici
sight
workir
that d
   The
notwi
100 to
tion fo
12 ton
   Dur
have b
deficit
from :

The Cornishman 11.8.1892

*In Bottrell's Traditions Vol 1 (1870) Captn Mathy visits the white witch An Maggey,
who recommends he make a witch bottle targeted at those who have ill wished his ailing
cattle: 'When the villagers hear about the witch bottle they all started to panic: "Good
lord," said they all, "we don't know, any of us, but we may have ill-wished the cussed
breachy things in the evil hour and minutes, and now we shall all suffer—God knows
what—through the scheming of old Marget and he."'*

*The following account is comparable to Bottrell's, except in this case the bottles cause
'bedlying':*

THE BOTTLE AND PIN CHARM.
The Spell Removed And The Spellbound Better.

'When will a belief in witchcraft, the evil eye, ill-wishing, and other *diablerie* die out in Cornwall?' is the oft repeated question among its more enlightened people.

In an old house near Brea, Camborne, this week, some bottles, filled with filthy liquid and pins, were found in a chimney that required repair. The bottles were smashed; and an old woman, who had been confined to her house for a long time, her residence being close to the chimney find, declared she had relief instantly the bottles were broken, for she was sure she was bottled-up by another old woman, who lived in the said house. (She, by the way, is getting a rough time of it at the hands of believers in the Black Art.)

The poor old crone, thus suspected, vehemently protests her freedom from any malice whatever toward her neighbours or anyone else; and avers that she had no knowledge of any bottles being lodged in her chimney.

The old woman who has been a sufferer for so long a time has since, owing to her joy at the discovery and destruction of the bottles, and at her triumph over her suspected foe, been able to jump around in her garden like a young girl!

There is another believer in ill-wishing, who is very ill in the same hamlet and he is anxious to find out who has "bottled him up; or he is sure that he is thus treated and that someone in the village has done him that fearful injury." What unprofessional white witch will find his malign bottles; or what professional sorcerer will, for a consideration, remove the spell?

What we have to assume is a different version of the same story appeared in the Cornubian Times three years later:

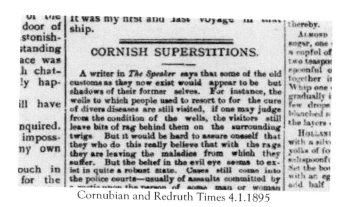

Cornubian and Redruth Times 4.1.1895

CORNISH SUPERSTITIONS.

A writer in The Speaker says that some of the old customs as they now exist would appear to be but shadows of their former selves. For instance, the wells to which people used to resort to for the cure of divers diseases are still visited, if one may judge from the condition of the wells, the visitors still leave bits of rag behind them on the surrounding twigs. But it would be hard to assure oneself that they who do this really believe that with the rags they are leaving the maladies from which they suffer.

But the belief in the evil eye seems to exist in quite a robust state. Cases still come into the police courts-usually of assaults committed by a rustic upon the person of some man or woman whom he believes to have ill-wished himself or his pigs. But a more elaborate story came to light the other day. In one or two semi-detached cottages in a small village among the mines there lived an oldish woman who had taken a strong dislike to her neighbour, the wife of a miner. The miner's wife, said sympathetic rumour, was a peaceful and respectable woman; she had trouble to live, because of the persecutions and vilifications of her neighbour. Finally she became a bedlier.

People often do become bedliers in Cornwall if they happen to be tired, and yet are unable to contract any of the diseases commonly recognised by the medical profession; there is hardly a village but can produce someone who has proved through twenty years, it may be, how delightfully the wind is tempered to the lamb thus shorn of the ordinary responsibilities of life; but the miner's wife was most unwilling to do thus, having a husband and a family to look after.

After some years the neighbour left: the miner's wife continued to lie a-bed. Then, for some reason or other, masons came to the next house and tore out the fire-place. Somewhere at the back they discovered some bottles filled with filthy liquid and holding a number of pins. These they smashed, and then-it is impossible to discover how soon, or at whose suggestion-the woman discovered that her strength had come back to her It is said that there was a young man of the village, himself unfortunately a bed-lier, who, when he heard the story, became convinced that he also was laid aside because he had been bottled up. One would like to be able to say that his friends straight- way organised a search for the bottles; they might have made sure of finding them, had they taken proper precautions, and bed-lying is the sort of complaint which ought to be peculiarly susceptible to the faith-cure. It would only be possible-certainly it would only tolerated-among an imaginative people.

On March 3ʳᵈ 1898 a fresh report, also emanating from Brea, appeared in The Cornishman. Then in 1906, yet another account was published:

The story was that Mary Baragwanath had been a healthy woman and a notable housewife. She had lived with her family in a semi-detached cottage. Her neighbour was a widow, with whom she "had trouble to live." At last she was taken with a mysterious malady, and though she longed to be down in her kitchen she was compelled for some years to keep her bed. No doctor could diagnose her disease or give her any relief from the deadly weakness which oppressed her.

After a time the widow left her cottage, and for a while it stood vacant. Then a new tenant was coming in, and workmen were sent by the landlord to execute a few necessary repairs and alterations. Hidden at the back of the stove they found certain bottles tightly corked, and containing a number of pins in filthy water. They knew what had happened, and they went straightway into the garden and smashed these bottles. Then they paid a visit to the house of the bedlier, and told her of what they had discovered, and of how they had treated the bottles. The woman at once realised that she had been "bottled up" by her malignant neighbour, and already felt that the spell had been removed. When her husband came home from the mine that night there was a rather extravagant supper, and it was the first that his wife had cooked for years.

At the same time, there was in the village-a little huddle of a place under the shadow of Carn Brea-a comparatively young man, who was also a bed-lier. When he heard this story he became convinced that he, too, was "bottled-up." I have always wondered why his doctor did not contrive to discover bottles under his very pillow, or buried in the cabbage-plot, and smash them and make him well, but nothing of the kind seems to have been done.

Local Preachers (1894)

It seems that, towards the close of the century, it was noted on more than one occasion that local Methodist preachers helped breed superstition. In 1894 the following short piece appeared in The Cornishman:

MR. C. V. Thomas considers cultured local-preachers are not wanted by Methodism. Yet Mr. Thomas, who is regarded as one of the most able and fluent "locals" in the county, is always in demand, and is appreciated by every class of audience! Culture is certainly not wanted at the expense of earnestness and good example ; but if it will bring enlightenment, and prevent local-preachers making some of the astounding and indefensible statements I have sometimes listened to, we can afford to take a liberal dose of it in Cornwall. It may also prevent local-preachers believing in the efficacy of charms and ill-wishing, of which class a few specimens still survive in our towns and villages. If the main sphere of preaching is to appeal to the heart it would, perhaps, be well if local-preachers, whether cultured or uncultured, taught little else than the beauty and need of living the Christ-life.

The Cornishman 8.3.1894. Comment in a mixed column by 'The Major'.

MR. C. V. Thomas considers cultured local-preachers are not wanted by Methodism. Yet Mr. Thomas, who is regarded as one of the most able and fluent "locals" in the county, is always in demand, and is appreciated by every class of audience!

Culture is certainly not wanted at the expense of earnestness and good example; but if it will bring enlightenment, and prevent local-preachers making some of the astounding and indefensible statements I have sometimes listened to, we can afford to take a liberal dose of it in Cornwall. It may also prevent local-preachers believing in the efficacy of charms and ill-wishing, of which class a few specimens still survive in our towns and villages. If the main sphere of preaching is to appeal to the heart it would, perhaps, be well if local-preachers, whether cultured or uncultured, taught little else than the beauty and need of living the Christ-life.

Gross imposture at Lelant (1894)

As this article reminds us, William Rapson Oates, though claiming to be a herbalist, already had a reputation as a swindler, and had spent several years behind bars (see Superstition and Swindling, Feock (1868)).

Cornishman 1.2.1894

THE GROSS IMPOSTURE AT LELANT.

A BELIEF IN WITCHCRAFT EXISTS:
(And to a Much Larger Extent than is Generally Supposed.)

At the Assizes, on Friday, William Rapson Oates, 52, herbalist, was indicted for obtaining 8s from Mary Sedgman by false pretences at Lelant; and also with pretending to exercise witchcraft and sorcery...

..December 29th prisoner visited Mary Sedgman, and told her that her daughter, who was seriously ill was under a spell, and that he had the power of finding out the person who had cast it. He was Dr. Thomas, and a brother of the famous wizard of that name, who resided at St.

Austell. After observing that he worked by the aid of stars and planets he borrowed 3s. from Mrs. Sedgman.

On the following day he called again, and mentioned that he had cured a cow, which was under a spell, for Mr. Stephen Polkinhorne, a farmer, and employer of the husband of the prosecutrix. Having borrowed 5s. which he promised to repay out of the £20 to be given him by Mr. Polkinhorne, he said the woman who had cast the spell would come to the house on a certain day, and that he would follow and exert his influence over her.

Subsequently he endeavoured to borrow another five shillings, but the prosecutrix became suspicious, and refused to lend any more money. When arrested prisoner told P.S. Hodge he thought the women were treacherous, and he supposed he would have to go to gaol for what he had done...

...The jury found prisoner guilty, and his LORDSHIP said Oates had taken a cruel advantage of a mother's affection for her daughter. From the records before him he found that prisoner began his career of crime 26 years ago, since when he had undergone one term of penal servitute for five years, and another of seven, besides several shorter periods of imprisonment. As, however, he had a clean sheet for indictable offences since 1881 he did not intend to send him to penal servitude. Very often it was difficult for a man to earn an honest livelihood after he had been in prison, but a man must struggle against that difficulty. By inflicting the lenient punishment of seven calendar months' imprisonment, he hoped advantage would not be taken of it.

White Witchcraft in West Wales (1895)

Gravesend Reporter (1895)

BLACK WITCHCRAFT.

The spring of 1895 has been disgraced, says the British Medical Journal, by sporadic cases of witch- mania[86]. White witchcraft has long flourished in those parts of the United Kingdom in which the Celtic race predominates, and in England it is still rampant in what used to be West and North Wales - that is to say, in the present Cornwall and South Wales.

We had fondly hoped, however, that black witchcraft was extinct, and that the treatise of Upham and the great bicentenary meeting held at the Essex Institute of Salem in 1892 marked the last phase of an epidemic which was once universal.

A distressing story of horrible cruelty comes from Tipperary, and upsets our preconceived ideas that questions of black witchcraft were no longer of interest to anyone but to the student of rationalism. A woman, aged 27, the wife of a cooper, has been burnt to death under the supposition that she was a counterfeit or changeling who, being hurt, would disappear, whilst the real woman, held as a hostage by the fairies or good people, would be returned...

---

[86] *The British Medical Journal*, Vol. 1, No. 1787 (Mar. 30, 1895).

A Child Ill-Wished (1896)

Mr. ROSVEARE.
A CHILD "ILL-WISHED."
Extraordinary Allegations of Witchcraft.

The CLERK reported that the surgeon of the Royal Cornwall infirmary had written that Mary Daniel, a little girl at present an inmate there from this Union, should, if possible, be sent to a convalescent home, or to the seaside. He (the clerk) did not know whether the mother could afford to keep the child, but he was told that she paid 10s. to a "wise woman," or witch, at Redruth, whom she consulted about her child, supposed to be "ill-wished," and was likely to pay more. He thought the Board might like to be initiated into the mysteries of the art, so he had brought Mrs. Daniel to the meeting. (Hear, hear, and laughter.)

Mrs. Daniell was brought before the Board and, in reply to the chairman's questions, said she never paid anything to the "wise woman," or fortune-teller.—CHAIRMAN: Is it true you paid 10s. to a "wise woman" in Redruth?— Mrs. DANIELL: No, I never had 10s. to pay. I wonder who could have said such a thing !—Mr. HOSKING: Did

This case was heard before the Redruth Board of Guardians, who were almost certainly paying to have a young mute girl placed in the Royal Infirmary in Truro, on the basis that the mother could not afford to pay for medical care herself. The mother might therefore have had good reason to deny paying a wise woman.

A CHILD "ILL-WISHED."
Extraordinary Allegations of Witchcraft.

The CLERK reported that the surgeon of the Royal Cornwall Infirmary had written that Mary Daniell, a little girl at present an inmate there from this Union, should, if possible, be sent to a convalescent home, or to the seaside.

He (the clerk) did not know whether the mother could afford to keep the child, but he was told that she paid 10s. to a "wise woman," or witch, at Redruth, whom she consulted about her child, supposed to be ill-wished, and was likely to pay more. He thought the Board might like to be initiated into the mysteries of the art, so he had brought Mrs. Daniel to the meeting. (Hear, hear, and laughter.)

Mrs. Daniell was brought before the Board and, in reply to the chairman's questions, said she never paid anything to the wise woman, or fortune-teller.-

CHAIRMAN: Is it true you paid 10s. to a wise woman in Redruth?-

Mrs. DANIELL: No, I never had 10s. to pay. I wonder who could have said such a thing!-

Mr. HOSKING: Did you ever go to see her?-

Mrs Daniell: No, I didn't-

Clerk: Not about your daughter regaining her speech?-

Mrs. Daniell: No, I didn't. I never heard at all of her until last week, and they said she was ill-wished.-

Clerk: We are getting at something after all. Didn't you see her about your daughter.-

Mrs. Daniell: The neighbours said she heard Mary was "ill-wished," and she asked me if I believed in such things.-

Chairman: You told her no, of course? (Laughter.)-

No answer.-

Nothing more could be elicited from Mrs. Daniell, and, after a time, she was asked to withdraw...

It was decided to apply to the infirmary for the girl to remain for some time longer.

Porthleven Fishermen (1879)

Cornishman 3.4.1879

If the Porthleven fishermen are ignorant and superstitious I would say that there are those who ought to teach them better things. But, Mr. Editor, where the carcass is, there the eagles gather. Charmers abound, fortune-tellers often visit the place and seem to do well, quack doctors drive a regular good trade, or irregular but paying trade, whichever you like. And if the poor people are ignorant and superstitious there are those who are vile enough to profit by the poor men's superstitions and ignorance and who can stoop to do any low and mean action to accomplish their ends. But ignorance and superstition are not confined to the fishing population of Porthleven. I think, as a whole, the fishermen of Porthleven will compare in intelligence with any men who earns a crust by honest sweat in this neighbourhood.

Why, sir, I once knew a man who had a mare as the man thought ill-wished, or with a spell put on her. And he put her to the conjuror, pellar, or white witch. The poor mare proved to be in foal. After her colt came she was better, of course, but the man never had the mare again. So you see that ignorance and superstition are not confined to the fisherman's family alone...

158

Palmist and Phrenologist, St Austell (1898)

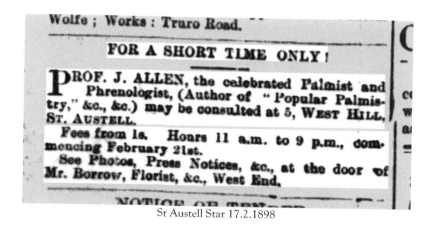

Wolfe ; Works : Truro Road.

FOR A SHORT TIME ONLY !

PROF. J. ALLEN, the celebrated Palmist and Phrenologist, (Author of "Popular Palmistry," &c., &c.) may be consulted at 5, WEST HILL, ST. AUSTELL.

Fees from 1s. Hours 11 a.m. to 9 p.m., commencing February 21st.

See Photos, Press Notices, &c., at the door of Mr. Borrow, Florist, &c., West End.

St Austell Star 17.2.1898

'Denied the house', West Cornwall (1902)

THE extent to which superstition survives in Cornwall at the present day is simply amazing. A case has just been put on record of an old woman, who on going to see her family in a mining town was denied admission to the house.

It seems that the family had not had very good luck in mining, and they came to the conclusion that this aged relative had ill-wished them. For this reason they denied her the house, and she had to take shelter with friends. Instances of this kind, it seems, are by no means as unusual as is generally supposed.

Mary Lee, Gipsy, Camborne (1902)

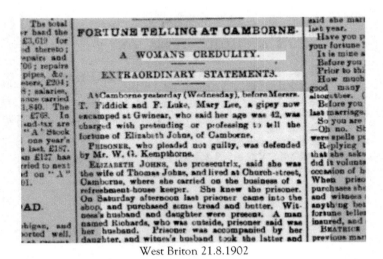

West Briton 21.8.1902

Reporting on a court case from 1902, The West Briton tells us that an Elizabeth Johns ran a refreshment house at Church Street in Camborne. One day the prisoner, Mary Lee, came into the shop to buy some bread and butter:

Prisoner told her there was trouble in store for her, and unless it was stopped dreadful things would happen before Christmas. Witness remarked, "Do not tell me that," and prisoner said "As true as God, believe me, I am the seventh of the seventh." Witness asked what that meant, and prisoner answered, "I am the seventh daughter of the seventh," and went on to say she was ordained, and that Jesus Christ gave power to people to do certain things. Witness replied she had read the Bible, but had never read that.

Prisoner then said "evil wishes have been made upon you....If you give me money I have power to remove the evil spell from you". (Laughter.) Was she willing to give her the money that day? Did she know what would happen before Christmas if she did not? Two corpses would be carried out if she did not put a stop to it. (Laughter.)

Witness said, "I am worried out of my life. Don't tell me of it." Prisoner told her she was under the spell of evil powers, and that her husband's people were the greatest enemies she had. Witness did not give her any money on that occasion, but prisoner made her promise to get some... Prisoner told her she would come on the following morning at 11 o'clock.

(When she returned) witness's son and daughter were present, and her husband and P.C. Hambley were hidden in a cupboard in the kitchen, and could hear all that was said-the door of the cupboard was purposely left open a few inches, and a mackintosh thrown over is so that they could not be seen.

Witness told her she only had half-a-sovereign, and prisoner said "Well, let's have that." (Laughter) Witness told her she thought it was sinful and wicked, and prisoner said "Well, my dear, God help you, and God help me." Remember what I told you to-day. Prisoner went into the shop, made some more purchases, and ultimately took the half-sovereign and suggested she should call for the remainder of the £3, and have it handed to her over the counter. Prisoner also put what she called a charm in an envelope, sealed it, said something about Mars, Venus, and Jupiter, and told witness she was not to open the envelope till the following day. When she took the half-sovereign prisoner took hold of her band and crossed it in all directions. (Laughter.)

Cross-examined by Mr. Kempthorne, WITNESS said she married her present husband in April 28th last year:
Have you paid very much money to persons to tell your fortune?-
Of course I have.
Before you paid this woman?
Yes.
Prior to this you paid another woman 10s?
Yes.
How much money have you spent in this way?
A good many pounds, I believe. About £15 10s. altogether.
So you are very fond of having your fortune told?
Oh no. She told me I was ill-wished, and there were spells put on me.

...(The magistrates said) seeing she had a child only four months old they would not send prisoner to gaol but would fine her £5...

Prisoner, who wore a large horse-shoe brooch bearing the words 'Good Luck' left the court declaring 'I am now going to tell her husband what she (witness) told me. She asked me to ill-wish him'.

John Taddy 'Wizard of the West', Twelveheads (1903)

Mary Lee, the 'gipsy' of Camborne, seems to have been an itinerant 'door-stepper'. John Taddy, on the other hand, worked from his own home and was well known in his community. In 1903 two policemen and their wives worked undercover to gather evidence against him. The first, PC Light, pretended to be a farmer who was experiencing 'losses'.

CORNISH FORTUNE TELLING CASE.

"THE WIZARD OF THE WEST."

A Well-known Character.

On Thursday afternoon an old man, known locally as "The Wizard of the West," was charged before Mr. T. R. Polwhele and Major Parkyn, county magistrates, at Truro, "with vagrancy by telling fortunes." He gave his name as John Roberts, of Twelveheads, in the parish of Kea, and stated that he was seventy years of age. He was dressed in the garments he wore when apprehended. He is of medium height, with prominent nose, effiminate features, and blue eyes. In the ordinary way he is clean shaven, but when charged on Thursday there were a couple of days' growth of beard and moustache on his face. His long, grey hair was tied by a red handkerchief, and on his head was a red felt hat. In his ears were ear-drops, a ring adorned one finger, and loosely hanging on his neck was an

had previously shown to us. Also a Greek testament.

Prisoner began to sing in a low tone at this stage of the hearing.

The Magistrates' Clerk (Mr. Adams): Do you wish to ask the witness any questions on the evidence he has given.

Prisoner: No, I don't wish to ask him anything at all. He told the truth now. When he came to me he told lies about the pigs. And the lady he brought with him told lies.

Mrs. Susie Bennett, wife of P.C. Bennett, corroborated.

Prisoner: She came with the man to have her fate altered, and said she was in trouble, losing cattle. Well, I said, if I can do any good I will do so. Those things (pointing to the glass ball, books, etc.) are little odds and ends — the rakings up from the world, the weeds of the world.

The second charge was then proceeded with.

P.C. Light said: I then went to the bottom of the garden and brought up Mrs. Kellow and introduced her to the prisoner. She told him her husband was in Africa, and that she would like to know his whereabouts. I asked him what he would charge. He said when he cut the cards he charged a shilling, and that he would tell her about her husband for 5s.

RCG 4.6.1903

A Well-known Character.

On Thursday afternoon an old man, known locally as "The Wizard of the West" was charged "with vagrancy by telling fortunes". He gave his name as John Roberts, of Twelveheads, in the parish of Kea, and stated that he was seventy years of age.

He was dressed in the garments he wore when apprehended. He is of medium height, with prominent nose, effeminate features, and blue eyes. In the ordinary way he is clean shaven, but when charged on Thursday there were a couple of days' growth of beard and moustache on his face. His long, grey hair was tied by a red handkerchief, and on his head was a red felt hat. In his ears were ear-drops, a ring adorned one finger, and loosely hanging on his neck was an iron dog chain, twice coiled. Under his long coat was a white apron. Besides being known as "The Wizard of the West" prisoner has often gone by the name of "John Taddy"...

On the table in front of the magistrates were several articles found in prisoner's house when he was arrested. They included bundles of letters, mostly from ladies, a large circular piece of glass surrounded with brass, and mounted on a rough stand, two packs of cards, a Greek testament, a sphere of glass about 2 inches in diameter, and a book in manuscript, entitled "The Crystall: Instructions how to use it. Very carefully copied from Barretts Magnus, etc., 1801." Besides prayers, instructions for the burning of perfumes, the names of angels, etc., there was a page representing a circle and a rod. It stated: "This circle you must make on clear parchment, lay it on the table, and place the crystal in the centre of it. You will also require two wax lights, one to be placed on each side of the crystal. You should have a magic wand of the form and shape of the following, to be used when calling the angel."[87]

Prisoner, when charged, replied: Not guilty before God and man. These letters were sent to me not by my asking. Superintendent Bassett said it appeared that prisoner had been carrying on the practice of telling

---

[87] See Appendix C for information on Barrett's 'Magus'. 'The Art of Drawing Spirits into Crystals' is thought to have been Barrett's own work, even though he attributed it to Trithemius.

fortunes a number of years. He thought it was time he was arrested. He therefore set a trap, with the result that he was detected in two cases on the 27th ult.

P.C. Light said: I am a police constable stationed at Grampound. Yesterday I went to the prisoner's house at Bissoe.
The prisoner: Happy day.
P.C. Light: I saw him working in the garden. After I had had some conversation with him he went into the house.
The prisoner: You told me lies.
P.C. Light: I had a conversation with the prisoner and a lady here to give evidence. I told him we had had losses and asked him if he could do anything for us.
The prisoner: You told me you were a farmer.
P.C. Light: He asked whether we had lost cattle, bullocks, or pigs, and invited us inside. First he used a crystal ball.
Prisoner (pointing to the glass ball): That's the one. A gentleman gave it to me of great honour.
P.C. Light: He used that ball, looking at the sun at the door, and meanwhile invited us to sit down on a couch in the downstair room. He then sat down and took a pack of cards.
Prisoner: That's true; that's true.
P.C. Light: He cut the cards several times and laid them at our feet, saying "Dark, dark."
Prisoner: Dark it is; dark it is.
P.C. Light: Dark it is; dark it is; death.
Prisoner: Dark it is, thank God; I thank my God it is dark.
P.C. Light: He found an old woman on the pack -the old woman which he considered had ill-wished us-and another card which represented death, saying we should have greater loss if the thing was not stopped, and that we should be out of doors.

The second charge was then proceeded with.
P.C. Light said: I then went to the bottom of the garden and brought up Mrs. Kellow and introduced her to the prisoner. She told him her husband was in Africa, and that she would like to know his whereabouts. I asked him what he would charge. He said when he cut the cards he

164

charged a shilling, and that he would tell her about her husband for 5s. I paid the money.

He took a pack of cards, cut them, and said her husband was living, getting lots of money, but living a gay life. There were three things for him to choose from - either to come home, send her money, or die. Prisoner also said "I suppose you would like to see him," and Mrs. Kellow said "Yes." Prisoner said "I think I can bring him home."

He further stated that the cards simply represented the 109th Psalm, and that he would have to do the remainder of the work at twelve o'clock at night by the fire. The cards were simply to see how things stood. Afterwards I searched him, and found on him half a sovereign and two half- crowns, the same coins he had just previously received.

.....P.C. Jeffery said he went to the house and found the three witnesses there. He read the warrant and told prisoner he was charged with fortune telling. Prisoner denied that he had been telling fortunes, and witness then explained that he had been talking to a constable in plain clothes.

Prisoner thereupon used fearful language. It was impossible to repeat his statements. The house was in a filthy condition. Two geese had been there some time, and the stench was terrible. A cat was chained in another corner. State of the place was very bad. Prisoner said he would see me in hell stewing in oil and treacle, making sweet soup for the devil, and he made rather worse remarks about Supt. Bassett, who was there also. There was a Greek Testament amongst the books, and prisoner could not read a word of it.
The Prisoner: You tell a lie there. Thank God, I can read every word of the Holy Bible as well as anyone in this room.
P.S. Jeffery: He has been carrying on these practices nearly forty years. I have had lots of complaints...

The chairman: you will be sent to Bodmin for two months in each case - four months. Prisoner was led by a constable out of the hall. As he went he shouted 'I shall die in there, I shall die in there: that's my last. You will see another trial of this. Much obliged to the ladies.

Fortune-tellers at Penzance (1905)

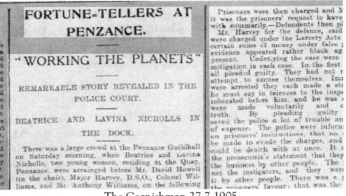

FORTUNE-TELLERS AT PENZANCE.

"WORKING THE PLANETS"

REMARKABLE STORY REVEALED IN THE POLICE COURT.

BEATRICE AND LAVINA NICHOLLS IN THE DOCK.

There was a large crowd at the Penzance Guildhall on Saturday morning, when Beatrice and Lavina Nicholls, two young women, residing at the Quay, Penzance, were arraigned before Mr. David Howell (in the chair), Major Harvey, D.S.O., Colonel Williams, and Mr. Anthony Williams, on the following

Prisoners were then charged and M it was the prisoners' request to have with summarily.—Defendents then pl Mr. Harvey for the defence, said were charged under the Larceny Acts certain sums of money under false evidence appeared rather black ag present. Under,ying the case were mitigation in each case. In the first all pleaded guilty. They had not r attempt to excuse themselves. Imm were arrested they each made a st he must say in fairness to the inspe roberated before him, and he was were made voluntarily and c truth. By pleading guilty saved the police a lot of trouble an of expense. The police were inform on prisoners' instructions, that no be made to evade the charges, and could be dealth with at once. It the prosecutrix's statement that they the business by other people. The not the instigators, and they were it by other people. There was a the prisoners' favour: that was the

The Cornishman 27.7.1905

"WORKING THE PLANETS"

....THE EVIDENCE OF MISS WILLIAMS: Miss Elizabeth Russell Williams, living in St. Hilary, said she had been living in her present house for three years. For 30 years she was a housekeeper for Mr. James, at Trelease.

...She remembered just after Penzance Fair last year that Lavina Nicholls, and another woman called at her house at Relubbus Lane. Soon after that Lavina called again, and brought a friend with her, whom she said was an actress from the stage. She subsequently discovered the second person to be Beatrice Nicholls.

She said the other girl would get witness's house back for £5. (This referred to a house of Mr. James, which had been promised to witness's child...)[88]

---

[88] It is later explained that Mr. James was the child's father, i.e. that he had had a relationship with Miss Williams.

Defendant was to have the £5 to 'work on the planets'. Witness gave Beatrice Nicholls £5. Soon after, they both called again, and Lavina said she wanted £20 to work on the planets, without which they could not get the house back. Beatrice said one in the family would die (meaning her child).

Witness was not willing to give them the money, and defendants then said the child would die. If they had the money, however, the child would live. Witness arranged to meet them at Penzance the following Thursday, to give them the £20.

Some little time after they called at her house again. Witness said she had no money, and Lavina said "You have gold in the house and we must have it." Lavina said "It is a watch and chain, and we must have it to work on the planets." Witness gave Beatrice a silver watch and gold chain which, they promised to return at Christmas.

....About a week after as witness was in her house picking fowls[89] a woman (Beatrice and Lavina's mother) called at the house and asked for a glass of water. Witness left the woman at the door and went into the pantry for water. When she came out the woman was in the kitchen....The woman said she had been before Dukes and Queens and had just come from America. (Laughter.) She said she would do witness good if she gave her £40. She was going to get the house back again. Witness told her she could not give her £40 and the woman then asked for £5. After that witness gave her £1. The remainder of the money was to be obtained the following week. The woman said "Get a good roaring fire in and I will put some powder on it." (Laughter). She also said she could stop conjuring and ill-wishing.

A day or so later the defendants (Beatrice and Lavina) came again, and Beatrice said "Oh, what have you done now, the planet has dropped?". (Laughter). Lavina rushed in and said "Oh, my God, what have you done now? You have left this woman come in, what are you going to do now?"

---

[89] Plucking chickens and ducks (for sale at the market)

Witness became frightened and began to cry. Prisoners then said the child would die, because the planet had dropped. They could make it all right if they were given £20. The £20 was to save the child's life. Witness agreed to give the money, to save the child's life, and arranged to see them at Penzance on the following Thursday...[90]

...Charged under the Larceny Acts, the prisoners pleaded guilty...Odessa Nicholls was fined £2, and Beatrice and Lavina Nicholls were sent to Bodmin for three month with hard labour.

A Soul Devouring Demon, Redruth (1907)

Welfare benefits were the responsibility local Boards of Guardians. In 1907 the Redruth Board of Guardians met to discuss the case of Eliza Phillips who had already, it seems, threatened them with a 'Soul Devouring Demon' after they stopped her 'out-relief'.

"A Soul Devouring Demon."

THE CLERK referred to the case of a woman named Eliza Phillips, Higher Falmouth road, Redruth. Some time back the Board ordered her out-relief to be discontinued, and offered her the House. He had considerable correspondence in the matter —mostly of a blood-thirsty nature—(laughter). In a letter connected with the case there was reference to "A Soul Devouring Demon"—(loud laughter). Mrs. Phillips was in attendance and wished to come before the Board, but she also wished them to understand that there was a "wise woman" in Camborne who would "ill-wish" anyone for 10s.—(loud laughter).

---

[90] Several more attempts to obtain money from Miss Williams are described here.

"A Soul Devouring Demon."

THE CLERK referred to the case of a woman named Eliza Phillips, Higher Falmouth road, Redruth. Some time back the Board ordered her out-relief to be discontinued, and offered her the House[91]. He had considerable correspondence in the matter -mostly of a blood-thirsty nature (laughter). In a letter connected with the case there was reference to "A Soul Devouring Demon"-(loud laughter).

Mrs. Phillips was in attendance and wished to come before the Board, but she also wished them to understand that there was a wise woman in Camborne who would "ill-wish" anyone for 10s[92] - (loud laughter).

THE MASTER (sotto voce): Ten shillings' worth won't be much amongst all this lot - (laughter).
APPLICANT came before the Board and said she wanted to know why her pay had been stopped.
THE CLERK: You must not ask the Board why they have stopped the out-relief They give no reasons.
APPLICANT said she was 72 years of age, and had worked since she was 17. She had never done any harm, and all the world knew it.

The Board confirmed the original resolution to offer applicant the Workhouse.

---

[91] Workhouse.

[92] Although greeted with mirth by the Board of Guardians this comment seems to indicate the existence of a 'black witch', or someone who was willing to issue baleful or malefic curses for a fee.

Palmistry and Phrenology, St Austell (1907)

In March Prof G A Wright is reported to have also given a series of lectures in Helston which 'attracted small audiences'. He also appears in Portreath, Redruth and Camborne. About two years later he published a similar advert:

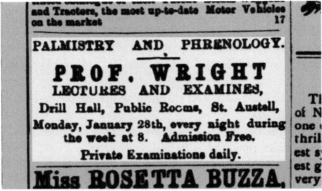

St Austell Star 24.1.1907

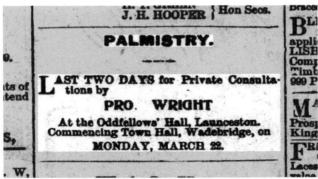

Cornish & Devon Post 20.3.1909

The Assault of a Dog (1908)

Though based on the recollection of the solicitor, Mr Thomas Cornish, the following account seems both reliable and interesting:

CORNISH WITCHES.

Witches (a term which includes both sexes) are well-known and constantly resorted to in West Cornwall. There are "white witches," whose power extends to the curing of ailments by charms, the discovery of those which ill-wish their neighbours, and not infrequently to the discovery of stolen goods. A white witch is, or was not so long ago, to be found in every town and important village in the district; but their powers are inferior to those of the more rarely-occurring "black witch." These latter can over-charm the white witches.

The late Mr. Thomas Cornish, town clerk of Penzance, and a solicitor with a large practice, writing in 1887 said that in his police experience he had had to deal with white witches at St. Just, St. Buryan, in Penzance, at Ludgvan, at Camborne, and elsewhere, and the best reputed black witch he ever got trace of was a man who resided at Helston.

"Some twenty years ago," he wrote, "a woman of Ludgvan parish brought up her husband for keeping her on bread and water for several days, and beating her. The husband's defence, solemnly urged by him in the police court, was that his wife's sister had ill-wished his pigs, and that he ill-treated his wife to compel her to induce her sister to take off the charm."[93]

About the year 1860 an assault case came before the Camborne magistrates. It was from St. Erth parish. A man beat another for ill-treating his dog. The dog-beater alleged that the animal had bitten his child the day before, and that he was only trying to get a hair or two out of the dog's tail because a "wise woman" (i.e., a white witch) had told him that the only cure for the bite was that the child should swallow a hair of the dog that bit her. In this case there of course occurred a curious continuation in practice of a belief which has in England passed into a mere proverbial saying.

---

[93] This anecdote is recounted in Deane and Shaw (1975)

Gipsies and Palmistry, St Austell (1909)

who is Max Barclay's
ours—the man Jean

indeed to you," she
were in my power I
e told me"
e laughed. "Why, of
ower to speak, if you

ssion to me," she de-
sacred."
exclaimed, regarding
garding her father, I

lf."
of a woman's weakness

terial," she responded
'as her most intimate
i in me.'
erns her personally you

r. Statham, and I will
t reflects upon another

ually so loyal to each
not without a touch of
r to be unlike all the

n anybody else. I sup-
" Every woman must
of what is right and

m do," the old man
s a subject upon which

GIPSIES AND PALMISTRY.

FORTUNE TELLING at St. AUSTELL

At St. Austell Police-court before Messrs.
H. Hodge, R.N., and J. Lovering, on Friday,
Sophia Broadway, gipsy hawker, of Plymouth,
was charged with telling fortunes by means
of palmistry at St. Austell on July 13th.—She
pleaded not guilty.—Mr. G. B. Dobell defended.
—There were several gipsies in court.
Lilian Lightfoot, wife of Sidney Lightfoot,
clay, &c., carrier, East-hill, said accused came
vending at her door and when she said she
did not require anything, defendant told her
she (complainant) had a bad spell hanging
over her head. Defendant asked to be allowed
to step inside, when she would tell complainant something for her good She asked
complainant to put a piece of money in her
(complainant's) left hand and make a wish.
Defendant " read " her left hand and told her
she would be going on a journey which would
be something for her good. She also said if
complainant had twenty children she would

place of safety, and
filled with petroleum
Mr. John Mitchell,
R. Harris, and other
hay rick and threw p
view to preventing th
was a fair breeze bl
roof fell in those wh
were exposed to con
flying sparks. Fort
and none of the help
wind was carrying t
direct line with a
occupied by Mrs. N.
away, and fears wer
but no damage was
a large number of p
air assisted in the q
mises. The only li
perished was a valu
P.C. Brooking re
the night and again
sum of money was
the morning, but
then that it had to
it could be opened.
In the course of
said he was returni
Trednnick from Pe
the fire, caused, as
of the furze by son
outbreak to be too n
but as he approach
peared to be nearer
anxious, and feared
fire. He drove as o

West Briton 19.7.1909

FORTUNE-TELLING at St. AUSTELL.

At St. Austell Police-court on Thursday, Sophia Broadway, a gipsy, was
charged with telling fortunes by palmistry.

Mrs. Lilian Lightfoot, St. Austell, said accused came to her door with
articles for sale. She refused to buy, and then accused said "You have had
a bad spell over your head." At Broadway's request Mrs. Lightfoot
allowed her to come into the house. She then said "I will tell you
something for your good." Mrs. Lightfoot put half a sovereign in her
hand at accused's request, and was told that she was going on a journey,
and if she had twenty children they could not be reared unless the spell
was removed.

Accused asked for the half-sovereign, but ultimately accepted 2s. 6d.,
saying that she would call for the balance later on. Witness handed over

the 2s. 6d., and was told to put a lock of her hair and a pinch of salt in paper and burn it. If she did not give her the 2s. 6d. she would be ill in bed, and no doctor could cure her. Mrs. Lightfoot felt afraid of the woman, and got her neighbour to call her away as an excuse for getting rid of her.

Accused, who was defended by Mr. G. B. Dobell, denied the charge. The Bench imposed a fine of 5s and costs.

Mary L. Trenery, Penzance (1917)

West Briton 29.11.17

One of the most interesting and inventive of the magical practitioners from Cornwall,
Mary L. Trenery claimed to be a faith healer, and to work with a 'council' of 24
spiritualists that included Sir Arthur Conan Doyle. Interestingly this council helped her
'do the spell business'. As we shall see, Trenery made other claims, such as having the
skulls of dead soldiers in a box. Here follow reports describing two separate court
appearances on consecutive days:

COW SOLD AT SACRIFICE TO PAY FEE

AMAZING STORIES TOLD TO TRURO PEOPLE

A very interesting fortune-telling case was heard at Penzance on Monday,
when Mary L. Trenery, married, of St. Francis-street, was summoned for
pretending to tell fortunes. There were two summonses-one in which Mr.
and Mrs. Gill, of Malpas-road. Truro, were concerned, and the other in
which Mrs. M. A. C. Dawes, widow, living with her sister at 11, Agar-
road, Truro, was named.

The Chief Constable (Mr. H. Kenyon) said at the beginning of
September Mr. Gill went into a hairdresser's shop in Truro, and told the
man there that things were not going too well with him. The
hairdresser...advised Gill to get into consultation with Trenery.

Mr. and Mrs. Gill called on defendant at her house on September 16th.
Defendant said that Mr. Gill was ill-wished by a gentleman in Truro, and
the sooner something was done in the matter the better for them both.
She instructed them to go home, and on the next visit to bring three
bottles to be filled with what she suggested[94]. No charge was made on this
occasion, but she said her fee would be £10.

Gill gave her £1 when he left that way. It was a good job, she said, he had
come to see her, as at the end of the month he was to have met with
sudden death, and would have been taken home a corpse. (Laughter.)
This upset him very much. (Laughter).
Sold at a Great Sacrifice

---

[94] This is likely to have been Gill's urine.

Returning to Truro, he took his only cow and sold it at a great sacrifice to raise the money to pay this woman. With the three bottles and the £10 Mr. and Mrs. Gill again visited the defendant, who gave them a cup of tea and made them very comfortable.

Afterwards she placed them as if they were to go through a marriage ceremony, and with Mrs. Gill standing, with her hands resting on the Bible, she burnt three small packets of some powder.

....The powder having been burnt, the ashes were collected and carefully put away with the three bottles. Her story was that she would convey the bottles and ashes to a certain churchyard, that they would be buried with the dead, and that as they withered so his and his wife's prosperity would increase. (Laughter.)

Proceeding, Chief Constable Kenyon stated that defendant told them they had a committee of 24, and that she cooked for 18 persons each day. She attended meetings from midnight to 3 a.m., and from noon to 3 p.m. She was the "in medium," and they could not get on without her. These meetings were held in the Friends' meeting house; she wore uniform there, and as soon as she went there at night the gates flew open to receive her. She was a spiritualist, she said and "being the seventh of the seventh for the fourth or fifth generation she was endowed with exceptional power."

Continuing, the Chief Constable stated that defendant further told the Gills that the navy was in her care. (Laughter.) She had been in a trance for eighteen months, had seen both heaven and hell, and felt her children fluttering around her. Death would be no death to her; it would be only like a dream. She said she had been to France, and had taken the skulls of shoals of dead men. Under the table was a box, which she said contained the skulls and bones of the dead.

The Chief Constable, continuing, said the woman stated that she had the power to make Gill sick. She had been employed by the Government, and had received gold watch and chain from the King for good services she had rendered. (Laughter.)

The woman was an impostor. She was one of the most dangerous women he had ever prosecuted She had fictitious testimonials, which she showed to poor individuals to convince them she had wonderful power, and that she was capable of doing everything she said.

...The defendant pleaded guilty and would go to prison for three months.

CAMBORNE REVELATIONS

Mrs Trenery was before the Camborne magistrates on Tuesday, in respect of similar offences. The charges concerned Annie Smitheram, from whom £19 was obtained, Mary Jane Pascoe who parted with £14 15s., and Lilie Burgoyne who payed £1. Margaret Hannah Pascoe pleading guilty to a charge of aiding and abetting Trenery.

....Mrs. Smitheram said her mother had been ill for some time, and asked if she (Trenery), could do any good, and whether she thought her mother was ill- wished. Trenery thought she was, and said she would try and do her good. "I work by the will of the Almighty," she continued. "I don't make any charge, but I will take your case for £10". That amount was paid at Mrs. Pascoe's house the following week. Trenery's statement then was: "I will do my best to get your mother around." After the £10 was paid Trenery very kindly sent a chicken to the mother, and it seemed to do the old lady good.

Guarding Men and the Army

Mrs. Pascoe, of Carn Entral, paid Trenery a visit at the house of the accused Pascoe, and told her of the losses in cattle she had had.

Then Trenery said the woman had been ill- wished, and that she could remove the spell and bring her better luck. Mrs. Pascoe had three sons serving in the Army and one in the Navy, and Trenery promised to guard them for £1 each and bring them back safely; £4 was paid for that.

There was another appointment, and Mrs, Pascoe (Carn Entral) and Trenery met in a room at the Railway Hotel, at Camborne. There Trenery repeated the stargazer story about her father, who, she said, could remove the "black spell" from the cattle and bring her sons back safely. She actually asked for a 5s. war bonus, which was paid to her. (Laughter.)

There appeared to be an instalment or two due, and Trenery wrote and threatened Mrs. Pascoe to put the black spell on her if the money was not paid. "This acted like magic" said Mr. Smale, "and the money was sent by return of post."

Mrs. Burgoyne had had some domestic trouble; her husband, it was alleged, not being kind to her. Trenery said she could "settle things" and "quieten him down." (Laughter.) She wanted 30s, for that, and was paid 10s, on account. Later she was loaned £1 by Mrs. Pascoe to pay this instalment, and up to now it had not been paid back.

Trenery had told Mrs. Pascoe that they had a committee of 24, who met at midnight until 4 a.m., and then all the spell business was done. (Laughter.) Trenery wrote several other letters to Mrs. Pascoe. In one she said the committee had formed the highest opinion for her (Mrs. Pascoe's) benefit, and that the course of instruction she desired would be most diligently carried out.

Mrs. Pascoe did not send along some instalments, and several letters were received from Trenery, some signed Sir Conan Doyle, and in one she threatened that she would cast "black spell" over her.

...Trenery declared that she had done no harm, and she had done good for many. She worked by faith and nothing else. She had lost a dear boy in the army, brothers and two husbands.

...Trenery was sentenced to three months with hard labour, the term to be served after the Penzance sentence.

Nurse turns Palmist, Falmouth (1919)

:APS

NURSE TURNS PALMIST

GARI

S ARE

AMUSING PASSAGES IN FALMOUTH CASE

A

AMME

' nearly a
all is as
ection of
ost of the
being St.
and with
iemployed
heard the

vernment
the delay,

There were some amusing passages at Fal-
mouth Police Court, on Monday, when Mildred
Ashby, described as a professional palmist, of
London, was summoned for using the subtle
craft of palmistry to deceive and impose.—
Defendant pleaded not guilty.

Supt. Nicholls said defendant was charged
under the Vagrancy Act. Since she had been
at Falmouth defendant had been most persistent in wanting to "read people's hands," stating that she was a professional palmist. In
one case she told a young lady that she (the
young lady) was straightforward, not easily led,
lost friends by being too sensitive, had a tend-

The
is grow
ing.
misund
when a
Two
grievan
got ba
could n
a piece
urge a
borough
cu or
authori
They s
the way
their w
take a

West Briton 18.9.1919

There were some amusing passages at Falmouth Police Court, on
Monday, when Mildred Ashby, described as a professional palmist, of
London, was summoned for using the subtle craft of palmistry to deceive
and impose. - Defendant pleaded not guilty.

Supt. Nicholls said defendant was charged under the Vagrancy Act. Since
she had been at Falmouth defendant had been most persistent in
wanting to "read people's hands," stating that she was a professional
palmist.

In one case she told a young lady that she (the young lady) was
straightforward, not easily led, lost friends by being too sensitive, had a
tendency to consumption, would never be rich but fairly well off, would

179

be married and have no children, was very thorough, suffered from nervousness, asthma and bronchitis, &c.

Another lady was informed that she bore troubles secretly, should have a great deal of trouble between 25 and 32 years of age, a happy married life with two children, would be left a widow at 40 and would live until she was 60.

Defendant had called at a well-known Falmouth Home three times, and so persistent was she that eventually one of the nurses, to get rid of her, allowed her to read her hand, for which 3s. was paid....

....The Defendant was found guilty and was liable to a fine of £25 or three months imprisonment.

Mary Hearne, Gipsy[95], St Mawes (1927)

Whereas many gipsy fortune-tellers were not already known to their clients, one, Mary Hearne, definitely was. Hearne and Richard Paddy had been acquainted for over twenty years. Versions of this story appeared in several Cornish papers, and in others elsewhere across the country. The following short account is from the Tyneside based 'Shields Daily News':

Shields Daily News 28.10.1927

"WHITE WITCH"
Aged Gipsy Woman Sent to Prison.

"She pretended that the illness from which he was suffering was due to his being over-looked by the 'evil eye.' In effect she said she was a white witch and that she cured the black magic which was causing the illness."

---

[95] All the newspapers describe Mary Hearne as being a gipsy, with the West Briton referring to her as being of 'no fixed abode'.

"This statement was made by counsel prosecuting in a case heard at Cornwall Assizes, at Bodmin yesterday, in which Mary Hearn (68) a gipsy, was sentenced to six months' imprisonment for obtaining money by false pretences from an old Cornish gardener named Richard Harris Paddy, of St. Mawes. There was a second count against her that she unlawfully pretended to use "a certain kind of witchcraft, sorcery, or enchantment."

Counsel stated that this gipsy woman had obtained such an influence over Paddy that she had taken from him sums amounting to £500. Hearn indulged in a number of practices for her purpose, playing about with a compass over his head, making a sign on a door, and talking about the planets and Venus.

She said that if he did not pay her more money he would go blind, become a bed-lier and die in that way. Paddy parted with practically all his money, and through mental stress his illness became so grave that his employer talked to him about it, the consequence being a visit to the police.

TOO ILL TO GIVE EVIDENCE.

The evidence given at the magisterial hearing by Paddy, who was too ill to attend yesterday's trial, was that he had known the gipsy for 25 years, during which he had been in the habit of visiting her. Practically all the time she was telling him that, he was "ill-wished" and asking him to pay her money to prevent the ill-wish from falling upon him. This had the effect of making his heart bad and he got very thin and weak.

Hearn, a married woman, who said she had been deserted by her husband over this case, stated in evidence that she had known Paddy twelve years and that he gave her money sometimes once or twice a month to support her as "he was just like a husband to her." She did not tell the magistrates this because she did not like to confess her weakness.

The Helston Witch (1928)

Western Morning News (WMN) 4.6.1928

In 1928 an oil painting of Tammy Blee (Thomasine Blight) was found in Truro. It prompted this very revealing article by William Paynter, who appears to have travelled to West Cornwall to interview people who remembered her. He refers to them as his 'informants':

Tales of the witch and her clients include the following:-
About 70 years ago a woman living near Helston had a child affected with a mysterious sickness, to cure which medical aid had been in vain tried. As it was generally believed in the neighbourhood that the child was "ill-wished," the woman was advised to go into Helston and see Tamson Blight, the witch, who, it was said, had the power of discovering who had bewitched it, and of compelling them to remove their influence. A visit was accordingly made, and the woman demanded of Tamson the name of the ill-wisher. This she refused to do, but she described the ill-wisher in such clear detail that the woman "immediately named the sorcerer," and returned home resolved to "bring blood from her." Some days afterwards the reputed witch passed her door; so she laid violent hands upon her and scratched her arm, drawing blood. The story told

was that from that hour the child began to get well, and was soon able to leave her bed and play with the other children, free from all disease.

SICK WOMAN AND A HEAVY CAKE. "My mother," said my informant, "lived beside a woman who was very ill, and none seemed to know what was the matter with her, except that she was supposed to be ill-wished. Two neighbours one morning left the sick woman in bed and visited the witch to inquire what was the matter with the unfortunate woman and if there was any hope of her recovery. 'Give me sixpence,' said Tamson, 'and I will tell you all about it.' 'We have no money,' replied one of the women 'Oh, yes you have!' said the witch; 'put your hand into your pocket', and on doing so the woman, discovered a sixpence, which she had placed there some time ago and forgotten; it was given her to go to Copperhouse Fair.

"Handing the coin to Tamson, the latter said, 'Go home, my dears, your neighbour is all right: and by the time you reach home she will have baked a heavy cake for your tea.' On their arrival, they stated, they found the sick woman in the kitchen quite well, and cutting a heavy cake which she had made and baked during their absence."

A woman living at Breage (near Helston) suffered from a severe sickness, being unable to move her limbs, and as a result she was compelled to sit in one position by day and night. A neighbour one day informed her that very likely she had been ill-wished, and the best thing she could do was to go into Helston and see the witch. Being unable to undertake such a journey on foot, it was decided that the preacher (meaning the rector of the parish) be asked if he would take her in his dogcart.

At first he refused, stating that he did not believe in such rubbish, but later he consented and together they went into Helston. After certain incantations had been used Tamson informed the woman that as soon as she arrived home the one who had ill wished her would come to the door and say, "Is my little black cat here?" The homeward journey was continued and on reaching the house an old woman hobbled in and asked if they had seen her little black cat! Whereupon the sick woman got up from her chair and taking two pitchers went to the well and drew water much to the amazement of the preacher who departed mystified and upset."

PEOPLE BROUGHT ON STRETCHERS. A man living at Camborne tells me that recently he met a woman who knew Tamson Blight well in fact, her husband, when a child, used to be put to bed with her, while his mother went about her business. He relates that before she died she was confined to her bed for a considerable time. Sometimes people were brought on stretchers and laid by Tamson's bedside entirely helpless, and they were known to rise up and go down over the stairs perfectly well."

The following was related to me by an old lady over 80 years of age, who was well acquainted with the witch. In fact, she remarked that Tamson told her fortune when she was a young woman, and even described her husband before she had met him.

"When I was a girl," said the old lady, "my master suffered many losses, which he attributed to the malign influences of some evil-disposed person. Tamson's help was sought, and she advised as follows: Go home, catch the cock, put him under the brandis (an iron tripod in common use with fires on the hearth for supporting crock or kettle) and cover him over with a red cloth. Then call together all your friends and neighbours and give them plenty to eat, and before their departure let each one stroke the brandis, and the cock will crow over the one who stole.'

Returning home, the farmer did as directed, and each one in turn was requested to go through the ordeal. Now it happened that one old woman present refused, but the farmer, not wishing to be outdone, forced her, and immediately she neared the brandis the cock crew, and she thereupon made a confession, in which she stated that she alone was responsible for the ill-luck he had had."

AN ILL-WISHED SHOEMAKER. A shoemaker living in Camborne used to make and mend the witch's shoes; but, alas, she was such a bad payer, he informed her that in future she must get her work done elsewhere. "You'll be sorry for this," said the enraged Tamson, "and I will see that in a short time you will have no work to do." Then she left him, muttering.

185

A HELSTON WITCH.—A recently-discovered portrait, by an unknown artist, of Tamson Blight. An article appears on page 6.

WMN 4.6.1928

At that time four men were employed in the shop including my informant, who, sometime later, went to America and remained away about four years. On his returning again to the West he visited his old employer and found him packing up his few remaining goods prior to leaving the country. On being asked for an explanation, he said that his work began to fall off after Tamson had all-wished him so it was no good staying any longer; he had lost practically everything he possessed.

186

A farmer who possessed many acres, and was in many respects a sensible man, was greatly annoyed to find that his cattle became diseased in the spring. Nothing could satisfy him but they were ill-wished, and he resolved to find out the person who had cast the evil eye on them. A visit was paid to Tamson, who advised him to confine his cattle until the next moon was as old as the present one. This, she explained, tamed the devils within them, and sent them to a far-way place, where she would lock them up for ever. He did as commanded, "and the spell was removed."

Tamson advised another farmer to go home and take the heart of one of the animals which had met with a mysterious disease and burn it with fire in one of his fields at midnight, at the same time uttering some strange words which she gave him[96].

---

[96] *Shortly after Paynter's newspaper article,* Old Cornwall *journal published the following snippet about Tammy:* One night when Aunt Tammy Blight lay very ill, a farmer came in great trouble about his horse, which he said would surely die unless she could help. As she was too ill to be moved she called her little boy to her side and touched him, saying certain words. Then to the farmer she said, "If you can carry my child to where the horse is his touch shall cure it, for I have passed my power on to him for this occasion." He did as he was told, and the horse recovered. M.E.J.

Fanny Francis's Thunderbolt (1930)

FANNY FRANCIS'S THUNDERBOLT

"Captain William Thomas, of Perranporth, tells me that he knew an old Cornish woman named Fanny Francis, who had a remarkable cure for a bad leg—to rub it in "essence of thunder." This precious liquid was obtained by boiling a 'thunderbolt' (apparently a neolithic implement) in a saucepan for twenty minutes. The owner of the 'thunderbolt' was a miner at Pool, who 'lent it out' at 3d. a time! The Captain adds: "I

The Cornishman 13.2.1930

This interesting anecdote, taken verbatim from the book, appeared as part of a review of T.F.G. Dexter's 'The Sacred Stone' (1929).

FANNY FRANCIS'S THUNDERBOLT

Captain William Thomas, of Perranporth, tells me that he knew an old Cornish woman named Fanny Francis, who had a remarkable cure for a bad leg - to rub it in "essence of thunder." This precious liquid was obtained by boiling a 'thunderbolt' (apparently a neolithic implement[97]) in a saucepan for twenty minutes.

The owner of the 'thunderbolt' was a miner at Pool, who 'lent it out at 3d. a time! The Captain adds: "I knew the woman well and have heard her prescribe". The "thunderbolt" is new to me, but I have known men who have worn a steel ring on a finger as a cure for rheumatism, or carried a potato in pocket as a cure for lumbago!

---

[97] Polwhele (1826) tells us that in West Cornwall 'the boiled dunderbolt is a sovereign remedy'. Although he may have been describing a neolithic axe-head it is more likely that it was a fossil or 'belemnite' that he had in mind. There is an example in the collection of the Museum of Witchcraft and Magic in Boscastle. See White (2019), and Appendix D for more examples of healing charms.

188

Harriet Sarah Richards, Hawker, Wadebridge (1956)

The fear of witchcraft and ill-wishing was potent enough as late as 1956 to persuade a couple living in Whitecross near Wadebridge to part with several hundred pounds. The report explains that the perpetrator this time was a 73 year old illiterate hawker, whose methods, it seems, were very simple and direct:

West Briton 28.6.1956

Gipsy Woman Obtained Hundreds of Pounds From Farmer And Wife.

Before the Court was Harriet Sarah Richards, a hawker, who was placed on probation for three years...[98]

---

[98] Other versions of the story explain that she was judged as being too old for prison, but was also asked to pay compensation of £100.

On April 22, 1953 the accused called at the farm and she told Mrs. Osborne she was "ill- wished." She asked to see Mr. Osborne and she repeated that he and the farm were "ill-wished." She then produced a rug saying that it contained three wishes, and that if Mr. Osborne purchased it the evil spirits or spells would be lifted from himself, his wife, and the farm. "Incredible though it may seem." said Mr. Brodrick,"Mr. and Mrs. Osborne have sworn on oath that they believed it, and a cheque for the rug was made out and handed to the accused."

"YOU ARE ILL-WISHED"

From then onwards, said counsel, for a period of between two and three years, Richards visited the farm with spasmodic regularity sometimes two or three times a week for a period of weeks, and then, perhaps only from time to time, with gaps of a month or more between visits.

According to Mr. and Mrs. Osborne, the accused obtained from them by means of similar pretences more than £600. It was, however not possible to be precise as to the amount she did obtain, but there were 15 specific occasions on which she obtained money, including the eight in the indictment, and £295 in money was handed over on 14 of those occasions.

In addition both Mr. and Mrs. Osborne said that money received for eggs and money saved from the house-keeping which amounted to £200 and which was kept separately, was handed to the accused. Remarking that that accounted for £495, Mr. Brodrick said: "Beyond that I cannot go specifically, but you may think that even if it is only £495 it is more than enough."

The representations by which the money was obtained were, said counsel, very similar, and, in fact they might perhaps be described as "variations on a theme." The theme which was present all through was "You are ill-wished; I have the power to lift or remove the evil spells or spirits: I can do that by placing on the planets the money you give me."

Mentioning that in June, 1954 Mrs. Osborne had a child, Mr. Brodrick said the accused called at the farm a month later. She then said she knew of the birth of the child and added that if it were not for her the child would be dead, Mrs. Osborne would be dead, and Mr. Osborne would be in an asylum. She required more money to prevent that happening.

Early in 1955 after the child had been ill with a virus disease. Richards returned to the farm and said that but for the fact that she had been "working day and night on the planets" the child would be dead.

HAD 14 CHILDREN

That state of affairs, said counsel went on until January 1956, and in that time Mr. Osborne told no-one about what was going on. In January, however, it appeared that he woke up to the true state of affairs, and, as a result of what he told his brother, the police were informed.

On February 7th Richards was interviewed by the police, and it was clear from some of the answers she gave them that she did not believe this stuff herself. It was not a mistaken belief as to what her own powers were. She did not believe she possessed such powers at all, and she remarked that Osborne must have been mad to have believed her.

For the accused Mr. H. E. Park said that both she and her husband, who was 73, were quite illiterate being unable to read or write. Married for 52 years she had 14 children and, in addition, had reared eight or nine nephews or nieces. She had "something like 100 grandchildren, and there are, I am told, eight great-grandchildren." She had spent the whole of her life in a tent.

192

APPENDIX A
List of named Cornish cunning folk and witches
All are derived from the folklore record, including Paynter.
*Newspaper reports (or similar) exist
**Likely to be a fictional or legendary witch

Polwhele
Ladock Conjuror*

Couch
John Stevens (astrologer)

Hunt
Ann Jeffries*
Thomas___, Bodmin (moves to Fowey after being assaulted).
Jenny Harris (who was scratched)
Master of Arts, Callington (probably Frederick Statton)*
James Thomas (and Tammy Blee)*
Harriet King and Elizabeth Wellington*
The Pellar of Helston[99]
Witch of Fraddam**
Madgy Figgy
Joan of Alsia and Madam Noy
Witch of Treva** (turns into a hare)
Betty Foss (and her owl)

Bottrell
Lutey of Cury (who receives his powers from a mermaid)**
An Maggy (Aunt Margret), Zennor
The Pellar of Helston
Tammy (Blee) the White Witch, Helston[100]

---

[99] Hunt, like Bottrell, though not providing a name, refers to the Pellar of Helston as a 'him', ie being male. Jones (2020) suggests this is a reference to James (Jimmy) Thomas, though I am more inclined to believe it is someone else entirely (see eg 1802 'Terrified thief, St Germoe').

Dolly Pentreath
Old Joan, Alsia
Betty Chenance
Nelly Wearne and An Betty Trenoweth
Jenny Trayer, Pendeen
Witch of Fraddam**

Courtney
Exeter Pellar (consulted by farmers from West Cornwall)
Uncle Will Jelbart, West Cornwall (charmer)

Paynter
Mr Snow, Herbalist of Launceston[101]
Lyle, Launceston. (Thought to have been Snow's pupil).
Jan Taddy, Chacewater*
Old Ann, Lizard (Helston)
Old Ann, Delabole (charmer?)
Old Martin, Tintagel (cf L.J.Dickinson in Old Cornwall vol2)
Miss Burnard, Altarnun (charmer)
Betsy (Bodmin Moor) (Black witch)
Jobber Mail St Teath Black witch**[102]
Ann Fradd, Delabole (charmer)
Uncle Jacky Hooper, Redruth (Blowing House Hill)
Uncle Will Jelbart
(Paynter also refers to a Grace Clifton (from Gwinear) who ill-wished the mine engines, and was a pupil of a Jane Kneebone)

---

[100] Bottrell, who describes a necromantic ritual in Stithians churchyard, does not give us Tammy Blee's surname.
[101] Paynter drew on the records of Miss Barbara C Spooner for information on Snow, and other cunning folk. Paynter thinks Snow, though he lived in Tregadillet, may have also been known as the Great White Witch of Plymouth.
[102] Paynter thanks L J Dickinson for information on Jobber Mail (see Appendix F Dickinson's article for The Occult Review).

APPENDIX B

Summary of Witchcraft motifs in William Bottrell

Motif	Detail	Book	Notes
Becoming a witch, pellar or wise-woman	Lutey saves the mermaid 'Morvena' and, in return, asks for the power 'to break the spells of witchcraft', 'power over familiar spirits', and 'for these gifts to continue in my family forever'.	B1. 'Droll of the Mermaid' p64.	Bottrell suggests that Tammy Blee and J Thomas are descended from Lutey.
Counter-spell/magic	Capt. Mathy consults An (aunt) Maggy of Zennor, who suggests using a witches' bottle to identify who has ill-wished his cattle... 'scores believed they felt the pains which they say are sure to follow when such measures are taken'. The community turn on Capt Mathy and threaten to burn down his house.	B1. 'White witch or charmer of Zennor' p79.	This is part of a long and complex droll, that also includes an account of the piskey 'Skilley-widden'.
Bewitched animals	Old Katey believes that An Maggy had bewitched her cows and her dairy and had tried to throw embers over her, as a form of counter spell.	B1. ditto	
Bewitched animals and persons	Gracey Winkey believes her ducks have been 'begrudged', and so too Cherry the maid, who is 'queer in the head' and suffers fits (despite owning a silver ring charm).	B1. ditto	Witchcraft causing mental illness?
Counter-spell/magic	Katey and Gracey and others resolve to 'bring blood' from An Maggy (Marget), but Maggy scares them away by threatening them with a pair of old horse-pistols. She also curses Katey.	B1. ditto p89	

196

Counter-spell/magic	In order the reverse the effects of her curse, Maggy recommends that Katey visits the Helston pellar and 'tells him to give her the Abracadabra charm'.	B1. ditto p94	The 'pellar' is referred to as 'him' ie it cannot be Tammy Blee.
Visit to witch or pellar	Capt Mathy travels to Helston to visit the Pellar, and have his magical protection renewed (see separate table). Many from Cornwall and the Scilly Isles do this in the spring.	B1. 'The Pellar of Helston' p115	Several charms are described (see table 2). The notion of renewing protection is unusual.
Animals *not* bewitched	Tom Treva's wife believes their ailing cattle are bewitched. Tom reluctantly visits the Pellar (conjuror) but discovers that the real cause is some 'mundicky stuff' used as rat poison.	B1. 123 'Tom Treva's Cows'	
Treasure-seeking	After An Jenny dies, money belonging to her, and to her friend Robin, goes missing. Robin goes to Tammy the White Witch of Helston who offers to raise the spirit of An Jenny in order to find it. The necromantic ritual that follows is revealed to be an elaborate hoax.	B1.125 'The Ghost of Stythians'	Locating lost goods was a service offered by many cunning folk. Bottrell refers to this as a true story.
Charmer	Dolly Pentreath, Cornish speaker, was also known as a charmer and fortune teller	B1. p179 Dolly Pentreath	
Wise woman	Nancy Trenoweth, who uses the hemp seed charm to summon the ghost of her lover, lives with her grandmother Old Joan of Alsia who is a wise-woman and 'deeply skilled in the healing art'. She also tells fortunes.	B1. The Millers Daughter p191	

Fairy ointment/ Wise woman	Betty Chenance, whose eye ointment makes fairies visible, is described as 'a noted wise-woman'[103].	B1. The Dwelling of Chen-ance p206	It is fairies that provide her with 4-leaved clover etc.
Shape-shifting (& witch gathering) (Sabbat[104])	Betty the 'witch' (and 'cunning woman') transforms into a hare, and is followed by Squire Lovell and his hunting dogs to a gathering of witches. Here the devil (or 'buccaboo') reveals his name to be 'Tarraway'.	B2. Duffy and the Devil p15	This is a Cornish version of the Rumpelstiltskin story.
Counter-spell	When Tarraway disappears, a flash of lightning burns away the squire's woollen garments. The squire then calls for a pellar who nails horseshoes over the doors, and places the household under his protection.	B2. Duffy and the Devil p20.	
Becoming a witch, pellar, or wise-woman	After being abroad for many years Nelly Wearne returns to Cornwall. An old friend, An Betty Trenoweth, encourages her to become a wise-woman. Together they read fortunes, and make herbal ointments.	B2. Story of Nelly Wearne P49.	Nelly has 'outlandish dress and strange speech which she affected'

---

[103] The fairy-band stepped down most gracefully from the little window-seat, on to the floor, and were closely followed by pairs of the little ladies, and some few of their gentlemen, all bearing bunches of herbs or flowers. All walked in orderly procession, bowed or curtseyed to dame Chenance, and stood at a little distance behind her until some elderly fairy gentlemen, who closed the procession, came up and cast their herbs into her apron. I saw among them many bunches of the four-leaved clover (with which the ointment is made that enabled me to see all their doings). They brought her sprigs of agrimony, bettony, camomile, vervain, mouse-ear, and hundreds of other plants from down and moor that I don't know the names of. With these she makes her salves and charmed lotions.

[104] Bottrell does not use the term, and yet his description is very close to the Sabbat described in the witch trials.

Counter-spell	A man and his wife, believing their cattle are bewitched, make an image of Betty Trenoweth out of clay or dough, and run a skewer through its body.	B2. Witch of Burian Church town p59.	
Bewitched animals	Betty Trenoweth, coveting the animal for herself, curses her cousin's pig. The pig fails to thrive, and Betty is able to buy it at half-price.	B2. Ditto p62.	
Bewitched animals and persons	Betty Trenoweth curses Madam Noy following an argument over some eggs. *'Madam Noy was never well from that day and her fowls eggs were always bad'*	B2 ditto p64.	
Bewitched animals	A 'modern' witch describes going on her knees under a whitethorn bush, and *'calling on the powers to help cast spells'* on Jemmy's cattle.	B2 'A Modern Sancreed Witch'	
Visit to witch or pellar	Dame Pendar travels to Treen to consult a witch on how to drive the Small People (fairies) from her best cow, Daisy. She recommends washing her udders in brine or sea-water.	B2 The Small Peoples Cow	
Counter-spells x5	As a result, all of Mr Pendar's cattle become 'lean and lousy'. Conjurers and pellars 1) bleed the cattle on straw and burn the straw[105] 2) carry flaming torches around the fields with the sun 3) Force cattle through the flame of bonfires 4) Burn his finest calf alive 5) cut down barberry bushes.	B2 ditto p76	

---

[105] This procedure is also described in Hunt (1865)

Shape-shifting	A witch from Treen is asked to steal a baby from the giant of Maen. *To divert him she changed herself into the shape of a horse*	B2 Castle Treen Legends p134.	
Witch gathering (Sabbat)	Witches used to gather at Castle Peak near Treen: *'(where) they scampered up to the platform mounted their ragworts or brooms and took flight to Wales...'*	B2 St Levan witches p139	
Fairy ointment (or green 'salve')	An Pe (Penelope) visits Jenny Trayer, a wise-woman, in Pendeen and secretly applies her fairy ointment to her eye[106]. At the market she sees a thief that is invisible to others, and afterwards, travelling home, has several encounters with the small people (including using 'the adder-charm' against them).	B2 An Pee's trip to market. p155	This has elements in common with No.12.
Cursed by knockers	Tom Trevorrow, a miner, is cursed by underground 'knockers' after failing to leave them some of his 'fuggan' (pastry). Tom's wife approaches a pellar for help - successfully - and pays him in woollen stockings.	B2 Tinner Fireside stories p190	
Being cursed or bewitched	Thomas Thomas never recovers after he is cursed by a jilted girlfriend. She hangs herself but leaves her prayer book open at the 109th Psalm (the cursing psalm).	B2 The slighted damsel of Gwinear	Bottrell explains that the 109th psalm was also implicated in the wreck of the Sir Cloudesley Shovel.

[106] Fairy ointment appears in several other Cornish drolls (eg The Fairy Master)

Use of a love potion	The potion or 'philter' is prepared by the Witch of Fraddam for the young, unhappy Lady Pengersec.	B2 Legend of Pengersec p255	Lord Pengersec is himself considered a powerful sorcerer.
Counter-spell/magic	'Many persons, believing the lady (Pengersec) had evil eyes, pointed at her with forked fingers to avert their baneful influence'.	B2 ditto p254	His 'legend' has many other magical elements.
Life-stealing	Venna, another witch, prolongs her life by drawing the youthful vigour of children to herself	B2 ditto p266	
Visit witch or pellar	The Norwegian Viking King Olaf (of Norway) was converted to Christianity after visiting a seer or fortune-teller on the Isles of Scilly.	B2 p275	Bottrell compares him to a pellar or white wizard of the present day.
Counter-spell/magic	Many 'western villages' had a Garrack Zans or holy rock: 'old folks passed round it nine times daily from some notion that it was lucky and good against witchcraft'.	B2 p283	
Being cursed or ill-wished	At the end of Vol2 Bottrell describes two illnesses supposedly caused by ill-wishing. The latter case is disputed by the local surgeon, who shows it is due to simple laziness.	B2 p285	The local term 'sprowl' (meaning energy) is used in this tale.
Counter-spell/magic	...leaping (singly) through flames, is calculated to ensure good luck to the performers and to serve as a protection from witchcraft during the ensuing year.	B2 Mid-summer Bonfires p287	
Witch gathering	After losing a wrestling match, the devil flies away to a hut	B3. Prize Wrestler p9	Part of a story about the

201

(& shape shifting)	where 'hags meet'. *In the small hours of the morning they beat home in the shape of hares.*		parson ghost-layer of Ladock
Counter-spell/magic	A pellar called Lutey recommended that people touch the 'cravel' (hearthstone) with their forehead at stated intervals as a safeguard against witchcraft.	B3. Touching the Cravel P17	ditto
Counter-spell/magic	On the way to having their babies baptised, the mother would pass the omen of ill-luck on the right hand, as she would a witch, and appear not to see her.	B3. ditto	
Visit to witch or pellar.	Conny Trevail is considering a visit to the pellar but visits a druggist instead, for advice about her pig who she claims 'es like a thing bewitched'. She buys some medicine for the pig as its cheaper than a pellar would be.	B3. Conny Trevail p77	
Counter-spell/magic	Conny also decides to 'bury the bottle of water before night' in order to 'make the strollop who begrudged me to suffer torments'[107]	B3. ditto	

Charms etc from Bottrell

Description	
ABRACADABRA charm written on parchment and wrapped in 'curiously folded paper'	Not in the text Bottrell v1, but depicted as an image instead. Described in Bottrell v3 p191

---

[107] The story of Conny Trevail includes some additional asides - by a very sceptical narrator - regarding a) visiting the pellar at the end of March, when the sun is coming back, to have protection renewed b) the ROTAS square. These comments are largely a restatement of sections in Bottrell Vol1 (1870)

SATOR, AREPO, TENET, OPERA, ROTAS written on parchment and wrapped in 'curiously folded paper'	
'A gritty substance called witch powder that looked like pounded brick'	Mathy p118 comments that the powder should be 'thrown over the backs of the cattle now and then' to prevent bad luck.
A verse of scripture written in the form of a charm	
NALGAH charm with image of headless angel and two eggs and TETRAGRAMMATON written under it. 'On the reverse JEHOVAH, JAH, ELOHIM, SHADDAY, ADONAY. HAVE MERCY ON A POOR WOMAN'.	Bottrell implies that he possesses a version of this charm himself. In Vol3 Bottrell explains that a pellar believes that these are two separate charms.
'A small bag of earth taken from a man's grave'.	
A green salve of healing ointment.	
Blood-stone, milpreve or snake stone. Can be used to infuse water, to create an antidote to snake poison.	This is most likely to have been a glass bead, suitable for wearing a charm around the neck[108]. (Not clear whether the blood-stone is different again).
Bring ill-wished beast into ploughed field. Bleed it on straw. As blood and straw are burning witch will appear.	Mathy comments 'many burn a calf half alive to save the rest of their stock'
Planetary signs for Sun Jupiter and Venus followed by a cross & pentagram and words 'whosoever beareth these tokens will be fortunate and need fear no evil'	An additional charm only in Bottrell Vol3. P191.
'Holding two forked (spread) fingers towards a person that has evil eyes is believed to be a safeguard from their blasting influence'.	An additional charm only in Bottrell Vol3. P191.

* An additional charm only in Bottrell Vol3. P191.

---

[108] Penlee House in Penzance has an example of an Iron Age 'adder's bead' that was found near Boscawen Un. It is pale in colour and has a yellow snaking design around its edge.

Illustration from Francis Barrett's 'The Magus' or Celestial Intelligencer (1801)

According to the *Royal Cornwall Gazette* (1903), John Taddy (see 'Wizard of the West', Twelveheads) owned a booklet or manuscript copied from Francis Barrett's 'The Magus' (1801) titled: "The Crystall: Instructions how to use it". The newspaper article hints at the elaborate preparation required of a would-be necromancer: 'This circle you must make on clear parchment, lay it on the table, and place the crystal in the centre of it. You will also require two wax lights, one to be placed on each side of the crystal. You should have a magic wand of the form and shape of the following, to be used when calling the angel'.[109].

This, in fact, is true to Barrett's original work, which includes drawings of the lights (candles), the wand, and the housing of the crystal which is to be engraved with the name of four angels (see illustration). Indeed according to Barrett the crystal is to be partly encased in gold, and to also rest on an especially made table:

PROCURE of a lapidary good clear pellucid crystal, of the bigness of a small orange, i.e. about one inch and a half in diameter; let it be globular or round each way alike; then, when you have got this crystal, fair and clear, without any clouds or specks, get a small plate of pure gold to encompass the crystal round one half; let this be fitted on an ivory or ebony pedestal, as you may see more fully described in the drawing... Let there be engraved a circle round the crystal with these characters around inside the circle next the crystal; afterwards the name "Tetragrammaton". On the other side of the plate let there be engraven "Michael, Gabriel, Uriel, Raphael;" which are the four principal angels ruling over the Sun, Moon, Venus and Mercury; but on the table on which the crystal stands the following names, characters, &c. must be drawn in order.

First, The names of the seven planets and angels ruling them, with their seals or characters. The names of the four kings of the four corners of the earth[110]. Let them be all written within a double circle, with a triangle on

---

[109] Barrett's 'The Magus (or Celestial Intelligencer)' (1801) is a much larger work which includes a section inspired by the influential Abbot Trithemius of Spanheim, or Johannes Trithemius (b1462). Although Barrett implies this is Trithemius' method, in fact 'the art of drawing spirits into crystals &c' appears to be Barrett's own invention.

[110] The 'Four Kings of the Four Corners of the Earth', according to Agrippa, are Oriens in the East, Paimon (or Paymon) in the West, Egyn in the North, and Amaymon in the South.

a table; on which place the crystal on its pedestal: this being done, thy table is complete.

According to Barrett, once the preparations are complete, prayers and invocations are used to draw benevolent angels into the crystal, whereby questions can be asked of them.

A modern recreation of Barrett's crystal ball, with its housing and 'table'.

APPENDIX D

SUPERSTITION IN CORNWALL

This is an account of Rev. Rundle's talk to the Penzance Natural History and Antiquarian Society (as reported in The Cornish Telegraph March 16th 1882 - the same report was also published on the same day in The Cornishman). Elements from his talk later appeared in Margaret Courtney's 'Cornish Feasts and Folklore' (1890). Interestingly, Courtney's younger sister, Louise was present at the meeting, and contributed her own anecdote.

The Rev. S. RUNDLE, vicar of Godolphin, next read a very interesting paper on "Cornish superstitions." There could be no doubt, he said, that belief in charms and ghosts - the two most popular forms of Cornish superstition was by no means on the wane. People may be a little more chary of expressing their convictions on the subject, yet all kinds of persons down in their heart retained a very strong opinion that ghosts still walked, that witches can still charm and that persons can still be ill-wished.

A farmer, for instance, would refuse to take some parochial office, because in the discharge of its duties he was likely to offend some woman that had the power of ill-wishing his cows. People, however, whilst openly confessing their belief in charms, would not talk about ghosts till they were quite sure they would not be laughed at.

To begin with charms: it had been stated there may be a great deal said in favor of actual good being done by them because they generally ended with an invocation of the All-holy Trinity, thus showing a certain amount of faith.

His experience, however, was that there was no such kind of faith displayed: they said "If you could cure he, you can cure me." Members of a society like this should guard the ignorant against impostors, who swindled them out of their money, by stating that they can take off the ill-wish.

Two old women quarrelled separately about a flower-pot. One of them had a son, who was exceedingly ill. John Bostock, a famous white-witch of Exeter, happened to be on his periodical tour through Exeter, and he declaring that the other old woman had bewitched the son, said for 11s he would make some medicine that would make the curser's eyes fall out of her head. The 11s. was paid - though previously they could not have raised 1s. - and the medicine made. But the woman's eyes did not fall out, and the man was not cured. Enquiry was made after the impostor, but he managed to escape.

An old woman once told him she had been charming a kennel out of a baby's eye, and as he was of the opposite sex she could tell him the charm. It was to repeat "Two angels came, one with fire, one with water; in water, out fire."

The charm of the dead man's hand was very common. A woman suffering from a terrible tumour once told him she had walked two miles to lay a dead man's hand on it, but she was too late for the coffin had been nailed down. Soon after her husband died: it was his dying wish that after his death she should take his hand and place it upon the wound. However, she said he was too near to her, and, therefore, she could not do it. Shortly after a girl did use this charm, and supposed she was cured by it. The form was to take the hand, cross it nine times over the wound, and then as the hand itself resolved itself into nothingness, so also the wound would disappear.

A cure for sore throat was to take a piece of a birch broom and cross it nine times over the part affected. The woman who told him this assured him that she had been cured in that way.

Once he was sent for to baptize a child, around whose neck hung a little bag which the mother said contained a bit of a donkey's ear[111] and that this charm had cured the child of a most distressing cough.

---

[111] A correspondent to the Cornishman a week later commented that it was likely to be a donkey's 'hair' not 'ear': 'an ear would prove after a while anything but a sweet smelling amulet'.

Whenever a discharge of blood from the nostrils takes place a certain woman was told of it. Without leaving her house she was said to have such an influence upon the sufferer that the afflux ceased. She told him the charm consisted in saying a verse of the Psalm, but she could not read, and he was inclined to believe the form was, "Jesus came to the river Jordan and said, Stand and it stood, and so I bid thee blood stand in the name of the Father, the Son, and the Holy Ghost."

Coming to ghosts, the author said certain sounds in mines were believed to be the old miners working underground: and it was said that good luck had been met with in working in the direction of the knocking. Not long since a great many people on a Sunday afternoon assembled at a mine to hear the knocking, but after a time the "bucca" disappeared.

Mr. Rundle next mentioned that about seven year ago he was staying in a Cornish country house. He knew nothing of the house, but he felt an indescribable awe whilst in the bedroom he occupied, although he heard no noises, that he could not well account for. About nine months after his visit he was told that one of the servants who had lately come into the house fell down in a fit and by her screaming alarmed the whole household. After restoratives had been used she said she had seen an old gentleman wearing a wide-awake hat, a long cloak and list slippers come out of the room in which he (Mr. Rundle) had felt a sense of awe, and cross to another; and the girl's description was recognised as the exact description of an old gentleman who used to sleep in that room, and who was reported to have done exceedingly wicked things. The question he should like answered was why did he feel that dreadful awe long before he knew anything of the ghost story.

In his parish not long since a house was said to be haunted, and always having had a great fancy for solving such mysteries he resolved to pass a night in the house. Two persons in turn promised to share the adventure with him, but both failed: one said his wife would not like it, the other was afraid of catching cold. A third man would have accompanied him, but before that the mystery was solved in this prosaic way: A couple had married upon a fortune so very private that no one knew where it was. The fortune notwithstanding, they got into debt and were very anxious to return to their parents, who however refused to receive them till one night the couple rushed to them saying their own house was haunted. In all such cases it would be wise to investigate and if possible, to expose the falsehood.

In conclusion, he ventured to disagree with the late Mr. Botterell who believed these legends were dying out. He believed legends were now in course of being formed. These beliefs in ghosts and charms would be only told to those for whom respect was felt.

The paper led to an interesting discussion, the CHAIRMAN remarking that it was a most thrilling subject. - Mrs. ROSS believed there were no haunted houses in Penzance now.- Mr. MAGOR held that the belief in ghosts would die out as education became more general. Mrs. Ross remarked that education had resulted in developing a new form of the same belief- spiritualism. Some people could and some could not see ghosts. She was once staying with some friends in a house said to be haunted. She saw nor heard nothing, but her friends, who were by no means nervous or superstitious, believed they saw figures, and left not because they were frightened, but it was annoying. People differed in the powers of the natural senses why not in the powers of their super- natural senses ?- Mr. HOSKEN RICHARDS classed ghosts amongst those things which "no fellah can understand," and using charms was like taking medicine-a great deal depended on the faith of the patient. A former servant of his wore a charm against fits - Mrs. ROSS mentioned that years ago it was believed a procession of coffins used to pass down Chapel-street, and it was reported that a woman who saw it said one of the coffins struck her, and she died the same night.-Mr. MAGOR: attributed that death to shock.

There was a well-known case cf a man who was so frightened by a threat to cut his throat that he died although only a scratch was inflicted.-Mrs. ROSS believed it was impossible to say there were no ghosts-Mr. MAGOR denied that spirits could take a material form- Mrs. ROSS: How do we know that? All we can say is we don't know for certain-Mr. UREN thought the belief in ghosts, charms and witchcraft would disappear only very slowly before the march of education. Some believed now that just before Christmas a coach with headless horses and coach-men drove from Tremough through the streets of Penryn, and that unless people turned their heads in a peculiar way they would be spirited away.

At Trewarthenick, the seat of the Gregors, near Truro, the servants would not go in a certain part of the house after dark. Three or four years ago there was a haunted house at St. Just. Within very recent times a woman at Enys had a reputation for ill-wishing because the expressions of wishes in two cases - in one that a man would tumble off his horse and be killed, and in the other that a man's pigs would die and his cow wither - were literally fulfilled. –

Mr. MARQUAND related that in Guernsey a family, formerly prosperous, had been ruined by the cattle being ill-wished.-Mr. RUNDLE mentioned that the cases he had given had all occurred within the last four years. He might also add that epileptic subjects had walked round the church at Godolphin at midnight and then stood before the altar. In one case a cure was said to be effected.-

Miss LOUISE COURTNEY mentioned that at St. Just a young woman begged of young men as many pennies as would buy a silver ring, which was believed to be a cure for fits.- Mr. H. S. HILL related how he had seen a charm used for sore eyes - the lad's eyes being stroked with a silver ring said to have been taken from the hand of a man who was drowned; and mentioned that in Devonshire if a death occurred in the family the hives were put in mourning lest the bees should die.- Mr. UREN mentioned that he once saw 30 hives belonging to Mr. Joshua Fox, of Tregednex, tied up with crape because of a death in the Fox family; and the CHAIRMAN said as a boy he remembered that when old Mrs. Botheras died at the" First and Last," Sennen, the birds'-cages and the flower-pots were tied up with crape to prevent the birds and plants dying. There was also the practice of going to the hives, knocking and telling the bees of the death that had occurred. -

Mr. WILDMAN said one of his earliest recollections was seeing a woman stroking a tumour in her neck with the hand of a man who had died on the edge of a limekiln in North Devon. And he related how he obtained a piece of rope a man was hanged with for a poor woman who had walked 14 miles to Bodmin in the hope of getting it that she might effect the cure of her sore eyes[112]. Within a few years the charm of the dead hand had been used in Penzance, and it was said efficaciously.

The CHAIRMAN, in bringing the discussion to a close, agreed that education would only very slowly eradicate these beliefs.

APPENDIX E
Granny Boswell in the news
Granny Boswell's biography, and her status as a magician, is somewhat disputed. However the following four articles, which are typical of many others in the local press, hint both at her large family, her big personality and her difficult relationship with the authorities. She was well into her 70s when these incidents occurred.

Royal Cornwall Gazette 1.10.1891
DRUNK LYING IN THE ROAD. At the Truro city police-court on Tuesday, before Major Parkyn (in the chair) and Mr. T. Chirgwin, Ann Boswell pleaded guilty to being drunk and incapable in Tregolls-road, at 11.30 on the previous night. P.C. Nile said he saw the defendant lying on the ground, and thought she had been sleeping, but when he lifted her up she could not stand. He took her into custody. Sergt. Bettison said the defendant had been there before, and the magistrates fined her 2s. 6d. and 3s. 6d. costs, or 7 days.

Cornish Echo 6.5.1898
THE "MOTHER OF THE GIPSIES" SENT TO PRISON.- At the Police Court on Wednesday, before the Mayor and Mr. J. Grose, Ann Boswell, 84, was charged with begging on the previous day in Market Street. Ann Boswell, is a well-known personage in Cornwall, and is known as the "Mother of the Gipsies." She possesses a very strong constitution as may be imagined that at her advanced age she indulges in the pipe as freely as in her younger days, and can proudly look upon twenty-four grandchildren. P.C. Matthews stated that whilst on duty in Market Street, the previous day, he received information that prisoner was

---

[112] *This appears in Courtney (1890).*

begging. Prisoner going to Mr. Andrews' demanded a shilling from the assistant. This was refused, and sixpence was proffered. But this prisoner refused and again demanded a shilling. This was given her by the assistant who was in fear of the old woman. - Superintendant Beare said that prisoner was well known to the police and she had been convicted many times, principally for being drunk. At the time of demanding the money she was under the influence of drink - Sentenced to seven days hard labour at Bodmin gaol.

Cornishman 22.3.1906

CHARGE AGAINST AN AGED GIPSY.
ANN BOSWELL AT CAMBORNE.

Ann Boswell, an Irish Gipsy, was charged before Mr. Fiddick at Camborne on Tuesday evening with being drunk. Accused stated that she was born on St. Patrick's Day 1815. She told Mr. Fiddick that her husband was dead and gone to glory, and that a monument to his memory was erected at Newbridge, Penzance. Asked why she got drunk, Ann said she took a drop for her stomach's being but the stomach being empty she soon felt the effects of the "cratur[113]." The police who apprehended Mrs. Boswell said he had to bring her to the station on a "donkey shay." Prisoner had a basket containing 1s. 10d., 3 clay pipes and a tobacco box. During the hearing Mrs. Boswell begged to be allowed to smoke and Mr. Fiddick giving permission, the old woman puffed forth volumes of smoke and nearly filled the room. At every question she would curtsey in a most respectful manner. On her promising to go into the workhouse she was discharged.

Cornish Telegraph 26.8.1909

NEWBRIDGE.

"Granny" Boswell, well-known throughout the county as a travelling hawker, died at Helston workhouse last week aged 96. The body was subsequently taken to the gipsy encampment on the moors above Newbridge, near Penzance, where it lay in a tent for a few days awaiting burial. The funeral took place on Sunday in the little burial ground on

---

[113] Crater

213

the hill side, the Rev. Rogers, of St. Just officiating. A large number of people attended, and several hymns were sung en route from the moors to the chapel.

APPENDIX F
Cornish witches prior to 1736
All cases, which resulted in acquittals, are taken from the Western Circuit assize records (from L'Estrange Ewen, 1933)[114]

1581, 8 Oct. John Piers, a pirate apprehended at Studland, Dorset, being suspected of conveying spoils to his mother a suspected witch at Padstow, she is to be examined. (Acts of the Privy Council). Anne Piers was examined before Sir Richard Greynevile and others (Cal. of State Papers)

1655, Recognizances taken at the Summer Assizes. Thomas Clarke of Peranzane[115], husbandman; Robert Vincent of St Allyn, husbandman. To appear at the next to prosecute against Henry Howard indicted for witchcraft. Partyes each in 20l.

1671 Gaol Delivery at Launceston on 30 Mar., Isaack Pearse, feloniously laming Honor Teage by witchcraft. Fel Martha uxir eius[116]. Do. Fel John Score. Do. Both, po se, non cul[117]. [To appear at next].

1675/6 Gaol delivery at Launceston on 7th Mar., ind mur Mary Glasson, murdering of Isabella Hookin, daughter of Francis Hookin, of the age of 11 ½ by witchcraft. Po se, non cul.
1686 Gaol delivery at Launceston on 27 July fel. Jane Nicholas[118], committing witchcraft on John Tonkin. po se, non cul, nec rec.

---

[114] These court cases, which are also in Notestein (1911), are discussed by Kelvin Jones (2015). Jones also adds the name Grace Bettie from St Ives, who as an accused witch was conveyed by horse to Launceston. The records for the Western Circuit are complete from 1670 onwards only. Ann Jefferies, the celebrated healer, who was sent to Bodmin gaol in 1645 is not, for this reason, included in the above list.
[115] Presumably Penzance
[116] Meaning 'also accused, his wife Martha'
[117] Meaning 'pleaded not guilty, found not guilty (acquitted)'

1696 Gaol delivery at Launceston on 1 Sept. fel. Mary vxor Joh'is Guy, bewitching Philadephia Row. Po se, non cul. *Tried before Holt, L. C. J., it was deposed that Philadephia who vomited pins, straws and feathers, often saw the appearance of Mary Guy.*

L'Estrange-Ewen (1933) refers to two other mentions of witchcraft in Cornwall:

c1664 Dr Richard Burthogge (*An Essay upon Reason 1694 p196*) recorded that he had a number of confessions in manuscript (all original papers and well vouched) of "a great number of witches (some of which were executed[119]) that were taken by a justice of the peace in Cornwall above thirty years ago" i.e. 1664

1671 Thomas Holden to Williamson. A woman about Looe is apprehended for a witch. I am informed she has discovered that she was in the fleet when the Duke of York was at sea, and hindered the prosecution of that victory against the Dutch, and that she has been the cause of the Queen's barrenness and several other things, and that she caused the bull to kill Col. Robinson, an M.P. and J.P., because he prosecuted the Nonconformists, she being one herself, either a Presbyterian or "Baptize." She was discovered by cats dancing in the air, and inviting one of her neighbours to the same craft. Some say she is maze and saith and confesseth anything, but letters that came thence say she hath several marks about her where the devil has sucked her. She is in gaol; the assizes being near, I shall then give you a more certain account. (*Charles II) Calendar of State Papers.*

---

[118] Also known as Jane Noall.
[119] This, together with a 6d payment made by the parish to 'open the witch's grave' in Launceston c1650 (Peter & Peter, 1885) is, I believe, the only evidence there is of witch executions in Cornwall.

APPENDIX G
Modern Survivals of Old Beliefs by L.J. Dickinson
This obscure account of witchcraft in Cornwall was first published in the 'Occult Review'
November 1917. More than a decade later Dickinson wrote a similar article for Old
Cornwall journal.

...There is not really much difference between my friend the old road-mender and a Christian Science healer. The former has treated, from a distance, the child of my neighbour, for warts, by some mysterious spell, and the latter concentrates his mind on the health of a patient, and gives "absent treatment" to a person unknown to him.

In the old roadmender's case, all he requires is the name of the patient; and he never takes payment; You may give him tobacco if you like, but it must be on some other occasion.

Another form of mental influence, which is very common in Cornwall, is "ill wishing." To "ill wish," or to "over-look," is to injure by some spell or charm, and perhaps the power to do so, which some persons undoubtedly possess, may be explained if we consider it from a psychological point of view.

No one now can deny the influence of the mind on the body, and almost every one grants the truth of telepathy, even if they themselves are too dense psychically, or too weak in concentrative power, to receive an impression, or to transmit one.

It will be noticed that a witch, i.e. anyone who is credited with the power to "ill wish" or "over-look," is always a person of determined character, with considerable will-power. If such a man or woman takes an object, a sheep's or a bullock's heart for choice, and sticks it full of pins, and burns it slowly, "saying words," a spell that is, while it is being consumed, he or she is, all that time, intently concentrating the mind on injuring the individual personified by the heart. If the person thought of is impressionable and sensitive the evil wish penetrates the astral body. It may develop merely as a depressing influence, or it may affect the victim so much as to cause actual bodily illness. It is said, if the intended victim

216

is upright, and is also a strong character, that the "ill-wish" cannot affect him, for the soul is then like an armour of light, and is proof against evil influences, in which case the unused force rebounds towards the witch and injures him or her. Evidently St. Paul knew about these occult influences, for he tells his disciples to put on the whole armour of light.

Spells for good purposes are in constant use in Cornwall. These are cast by a "white witch," and their object is to relieve pain, to soothe the irritation caused by insect bites, and even to remove an evil spell. An old man, whom I knew well, worked his charms by twisting an ash or willow wand round the part affected, and "saying words." He was very successful in curing both people and animals.

In most cases that have come within my personal knowledge, I think the result may be attributed to the influence of mind on matter, but undoubtedly there are other happenings not so easily accounted for.

Some years ago an old woman lived near me called Mrs. Tregay,* who was believed to have "over-looked " many of her neighbours. She was a person of strong character and great magnetic force. You either liked her, or shrank from her in fear ; she had also great power over animals, and her donkey obeyed her voice and followed her about like a dog. Most of her neighbours were so frightened of her that they avoided even passing her on the road.

She once met her match in witchcraft in Mr. Hale, the "white witch" of a neighbouring town, who died recently. His ostensible profession was that of a herbalist, and he always used to attend the local market, where his remedies could be bought, and his advice obtained on more occult matters. The story of how he released a man from old Philippa Tregay's spell is well-known in the district, but unfortunately it is not suitable for publication; anyhow it was quite successful.

It must be remembered that a white witch uses his or her powers for good purposes, the black witch for evil ones. That is the only difference between them. This same white witch Mr. Hale was mixed up in another case that concerned a woman I know very well. Her husband had fallen ill with a strange wasting disease, which baffled the local doctor, and the friends of the patient said he was "over-looked," so his wife, Mrs. Crowle, decided to consult Mr. Hale. She invited another woman for company, and they drove off to the village where he lived. Mr. Hale was at home, and after hearing their business, took them into an inner room, and told Mrs. Crowle to gaze steadily in a mirror that he showed her, saying that there she would see the face of the person who had bewitched her husband. Mrs. Crowle looked fixedly in the glass, expecting to see Mrs. Tregay, for it was she who was generally thought to have "over-looked" Mr. Crowle ; but to her horror and surprise, the face that appeared in the mirror was not that of Mrs. Tregay, but of old Mrs. Crowle, the husband's mother! It gave the seer such a shock that she fled from the room, and hastily departed.

On the drive home, the two women thought over every unpleasant incident connected with the mother-in-law, but all they could remember as a reason for "ill-wishing," was a quarrel about some butter!

The curious thing to us, of course, is that a face should appear in the mirror at all, and I can suggest no explanation except that the mirror may be used as the crystal is by clairvoyants, and that most of the gazers are rather psychic. It is not very long since this occurred, and I have come across other cases where a glass has been used to discover who was the person casting the spell.

Pigs and cattle can be "ill-wished" as well as people, so that they waste away and die, and some envious neighbour is thought to be at the bottom of it. There is a farm which has always had the reputation of being under curious influences; in fact, it is still believed to be haunted. In the life-time of a man still living (and it was he who related the tale) it was "bewitched" on a very extensive scale. Day after day the animals were found dead, and everything went wrong. The crops were a failure, and even the butter "wouldn't come." At last the owners, Mr. Rosewame and his wife, decided to journey to Exeter, to consult a famous white witch who lived there. The witch was a man of extraordinary gifts, and his fame had spread through all Devon and Cornwall. Mr. Rosewarne was so much impressed by him (for the witch showed an intimate knowledge of his, Rosewarne's, private life, before any information had been imparted), that he engaged him to come back with him to the Old Cromlech Farm to remove the spell. This was done at midnight with due ceremony. The Rosewarnes and the "witch," all the household and the labourers, each holding a lantern or a light of some kind in the hand, perambulated the farm, going through every field, and into every barn and stable, while the white witch repeated psalms as they marched along, and "said words" from time to time, with the result that the evil spell was removed, and the crops and the cattle flourished again.

What the "words" are, which are used in the spell, may only be revealed on the death-bed, and then only to a person of the opposite sex. The charm cannot be handed on even from mother to daughter, but the woman must choose a man to be the successor to her knowledge, and vice-versa.

In but one case have I been able to ascertain the words used in the spell. It is a charm for stopping bleeding; the girl who told me about it had cut her hand badly, so that the haemorrhage was profuse. She hastened to a man that she knew possessed the blood-charm, and she was alert enough to catch the words. The old man took her hand, and said—

Jesus Christ was born in Bethlehem,
Baptized in the river of Jordan.
The water was wild and rude— .
Christ was mild and good—
He bade it stand, and it stood.
So may the blood of Mary Brown
In the name of the Father, the Son, and the Holy Ghost.

This has to be repeated three times, using the patient's own name in the right place, and then the bleeding will stop, which, according to my informant, it always does.

One would not expect these words to affect the circulation of a person, still less that of an animal; yet the same charm was once used to injure a neighbour, by spoiling the carcase of a pig he had just killed. The pig, a very fine one it was said, was slaughtered in the usual way by cutting its throat. A man, standing by, who was filled with envy at its goodly proportions, muttered this charm, and at once the blood stopped flowing. It congealed within the carcase, rendering it unfit for food, and causing considerable loss to the owner. There is nothing I know of which can account for this. Perhaps some student of the occult can throw light upon it?

In many parts of the world, gipsies are credited with occult powers, and certainly in Cornwall people are afraid of offending them. Sometimes they trade on the fear they arouse to make the cottagers buy worthless brooms and brushes for twice their value. On other occasions they just look at a person, and give advice or warning, without asking for, or expecting, payment. A few days ago a gipsy woman called at a little farm near here, and told the wife that there was money coming to her in a letter. This seemed most unlikely, but the next morning the woman, to her great surprise, received a letter with a considerable sum of money in it.

A disgusting form of ill-wishing by a gipsy, causing vermin, took place in Cornwall, and the victims were all known to me. A woman, called Mrs. Price, kept a little shop, and a gipsy came to her, urging her to buy her wares, which Mrs. Price refused. The gipsy became angry and abusive and could not be got rid of. At last she departed, and it was noticed that she looked very carefully at the name John Price, written over the shop door.

The next day, the woman living opposite, whose name was also Price, came rushing in, in great excitement and distress, with her baby little John Price in her arms. She showed the people in the shop that the child was absolutely covered with vermin, which was incomprehensible, as they were very clean people, and there had not been a vestige of such a thing even the day before. The only way the visitation could be accounted for was the gipsy's curse, for it is well known that an ill-wish, or a curse, if directed at a family, or indiscriminately at a name, always goes to the youngest, and the baby, little John Price, was the youngest of that name. No doubt the gipsy had intended to injure the husband whose name was over the shop.

Another gipsy had a quarrel with John Cardew, whom I used to know, and went out from his cottage in wrath. When outside, the Cardews noticed that she was making a "ring," or circle in the road, and seemed to be "saying words."

From that day forth John Cardew's youngest little girl ceased to grow. She was then about eight, so as she grew up she became a dwarf. This misfortune was always attributed to the family being "ill-wished" by the gipsy, and the spell falling, as is the custom, on the youngest.

It is always believed that running water has great power. No witch, however malevolent, can cast a spell if running water be between her and her victim, so if you have reason to dread the enmity of a "wise woman," you should go and live the other side of a stream. I have been told of several persons who moved from one side of the parish to the other, in order to have running water between them and their enemy...

*I have changed the names for obvious reasons: otherwise the stories are related as they happened, or as they were told me.

BIBLIOGRAPHY

Borlase, William (1754) *Antiquities, Historical and Monumental, of the County of Cornwall*

Borlase, William (1756) *Observations of the Ancient and Present State of the Islands of Scilly*

Borlase, William (1758) *The Natural History of Cornwall*

Bottrell, William (1870 & 1873) *Traditions and Hearthside Stories of West Cornwall Vols 1 & 2*

Bottrell, William (1880) *Stories and Folklore of West Cornwall (Vol 3)*

Carew, Richard (1602) *Survey of Cornwall*

Couch, Jonathan (1871) *History of Polperro*

Courtney, Margaret (1890) *Cornish Feasts and Folklore*

Culpeper, Nicholas (1826) *Complete Herbal & English Physician*

Davies, Owen (1999a) *A People Bewitched: Witchcraft and Magic in 19th Century Somerset* Bruton

Davies, Owen (1999b) *Witchcraft, Magic and Culture* Manchester University Press

Davies, Owen (2003) *Popular Magic: Cunning Folk in English History* Continuum

Davies, Owen (2013) *America Bewitched: The Story of Witchcraft after Salem* Oxford University Press

Deane, Tony & Shaw, Tony (1975) *The Folklore of Cornwall* Batsford

Ewen, L'Estrange C. (1933) *Witchcraft and Demonianism* Heath Cranton

Gary, Gemma (2011) *Traditional Witchcraft: A Cornish book of Ways (2nd Edition)* Troy Books

Hammond, J (1897) *A Cornish Parish: Being an account of St Austell*

Hawker, Revd Robert (1870) *Footprints of Former Men in Far Cornwall*

Hunt, Robert (1865) *Popular Romances of the West of England*

Jenkin, Hamilton A K (1933) *Cornwall and the Cornish*

Jones, Kelvin (2015) *Cornish Witches: History and Craft of Cornish Witches* Cunning Crime Books

Jones, Kelvin I (2020) *The Cornish Folklore Collection Volume One Witchcraft, Spells, Charms, Cures and Superstitions*

Langstone, Alex (2017) *From Granite to Sea: Folklore of Bodmin Moor and East Cornwall* Troy Books

Merrifield, Ralph (1987) *Archaeology of Ritual and Magic* Guild Publishing

Notestein, Wallace (1911) *A History of Witchcraft in England from 1558 – 1718*

Paynter, William H (2016) *Cornish Witchcraft* (written in the 1940s)

Peter, R. & Peter O. B. (1885) *The Histories of Launceston and Dunheved*

Polwhele, Richard (1803-6) *History of Cornwall*

Polwhele, Richard (1826) *Traditions and Recollections*

Pool, P.A.S. (1986) *William Borlase* RIC

Semmens, Jason (2004) *The Witch of the West: or the Strange and Wonderful story of Thomasine Blight*

Semmens, Jason (2008) *The Cornish Witchfinder: William Henry Paynter and the Witchery, Ghosts, Charms and Folklore of Cornwall*

Semmens, Jason 2011 *'The Trials of Frederick Statton MA'* Old Cornwall 14 no5

Semmens, Jason 2014 *'An incorrigible rogue'* Old Cornwall 14 no10

Thomas, Keith (1971) *Religion and the Decline of Magic*

White, Rupert (2017) *The Re-enchanted Landscape: Earth Mysteries, Paganism and Art in Cornwall* Antenna Publications

White, Rupert (2019) *Physick and Folk Medicine: A History of Healthcare in Cornwall* Antenna Publications

♈			B	B
♉			P	C
♊			A	D
♋			Z	F
♌			K	G
♍			Λ	L
♎			M	M
♏			N	N
♐			Π	P
♑			P	R
♒			G	S
♓			T	T
♄			A	A
♂			H	E
⊕			I	I
♀			O	O
☿			Y	V
☾			W	Iconf Vcos
Terra			O	K
Aqua			≡	Q
Aer			Φ	X
Ignis	7	↻	X	Z
Spus			Ψ	H

INDEX

N

Newlyn, 26, 44, 45
Noose rope (charm), 211
North Hill, 99, 100
North Tamerton, 25
Notestein, Wallace, 214

O

Old Cornwall (journal), 11, 13, 127,
    187, 195, 224
Old Joan of Alsia, 197

P

Padstow, 64, 75
palmist, 159, 179
palmistry, 19, 24, 26, 27, 95, 126, 170,
    173, 179
Parkin, Dr John, 24
paupers. See social class
Paynter, William, 12, 14, 77, 183, 194,
    195
pellar, 9, 11, 30, 80, 81, 94, 102, 127,
    135, 158, 194, 195, 196, 197, 198,
    199, 200, 201, 202, 203
Penryn, 16, 84, 104, 105, 210
Penzance, 16, 31, 45, 50, 91, 94, 95,
    120, 138, 139, 140, 166, 167, 168,
    172, 174, 175, 178, 203, 207, 210,
    212
Phillack, 55
phrenologist, 159
phrenology, 129, 170
pierced heart, 17, 63, 90
Plymouth, 42, 43, 70, 195
Polperro, 23, 222
Polwhele, Richard, 11, 34, 188, 194
Powell, Nathan (astrologer), 22, 24
preachers, 142, 152
Prof G A Wright, 170

R

Raffalonious, 144, 145
Raphael, 25, 26, 137
Rapson Oates, 13, 97, 153, 154
RCG. See Royal Cornwall Gazette
Redruth, 11, 12, 13, 16, 51, 67, 73, 78,
    80, 86, 87, 98, 115, 116, 123, 130,
    149, 156, 157, 168, 169, 170, 195
religion, 142
remedy, 55
reverse witch trials. See witch scratching
Richard Couch, 112
Richard Palmer, 25
Roseland, 81, 146
Royal Cornwall Gazette, 14, 15, 16, 17,
    24, 27, 144
Russel Bosisto, 145

S

Scilly Isles, 10, 31, 197, 201
seine, 44, 45, 83
Semmens, Jason, 12, 13, 51, 52, 57, 97,
    224
seventh son or daughter, 104, 160, 176
sick, 48, 97, 135, 176, 184
sickness, 31, 68, 183, 184
silver ring (charm), 99, 100, 196, 211
Sithney, 30
social class, 20, 74, 84, 92, 109, 115,
    142, 143
Society of Skilful Aunts, 10
Somerset, 20, 23, 136, 144
spell, 33, 46, 47, 56, 60, 66, 68, 71, 78,
    79, 80, 84, 85, 93, 105, 107, 109,
    116, 121, 130, 131, 132, 133, 142,
    143, 148, 151, 153, 154, 158, 160,
    161, 162, 173, 175, 177, 178, 187,
    190, 196, 197, 198, 199, 201, 202
spiritualism, 143, 210
spiritualist, 176
St Austell, 35, 42, 70, 126, 159, 170,
    173
St Cleer, 71
St Columb, 68

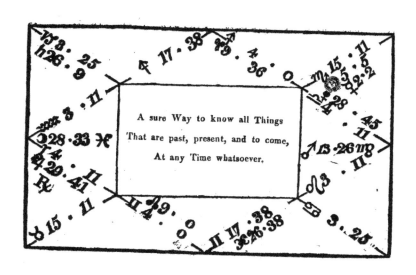

A sure Way to know all Things
That are past, present, and to come,
At any Time whatsoever.

231

Printed in Great Britain
by Amazon

45202981R00131